It's Time to Dream Again

It's Time to Dream Again
Copyright © 2024 Joel Osteen

Scripture quotations marked AMP are taken from the Amplified Bible, Copyright © 1954, 1958, 1962, 1964, 1965, 1987 by The Lockman Foundation. Used by permission.

Scripture quotations marked ESV are taken from The Holy Bible, English Standard Version® (ESV®), Copyright © 2001 by Crossway, a publishing ministry of Good News Publishers. All rights reserved.

Scripture quotations marked KJV are taken from the King James Version®. Public domain.

Scripture quotations marked MEV are taken from The Holy Bible, Modern English Version. Copyright © 2014 by Military Bible Association. All rights reserved.

Scripture quotations marked NIV are taken from the Holy Bible, New International Version®, NIV®. Copyright © 1973, 1978, 1984, 2011 by Biblica, Inc.™ Used by permission of Zondervan. All rights reserved worldwide. http://www.zondervan.com The "NIV" and "New International Version" are trademarks registered in the United States Patent and Trademark Office by Biblica, Inc.™

Scripture quotations marked NKJV are taken from the New King James Version®. Copyright © 1982 by Thomas Nelson. Used by permission. All rights reserved.

ISBN: 978-1-951701-73-4

Created and assembled for Joel Osteen Ministries by
Breakfast for Seven
breakfastforseven.com

Printed in China.

For additional resources by Joel Osteen, visit JoelOsteen.com

JOEL OSTEEN

It's Time to Dream Again

MOMENTS OF INSPIRATION

Contents

Introduction vii

SECTION 1: DREAMS

1. Buried Dreams 1
2. Remember 11
3. Light the Fire 21
4. Dream Big 31
5. Hidden Treasure 41
6. The Master 51

SECTION 2: CLEAR VISION

7. Images 63
8. Windshield Wipers 73
9. Grasshoppers 83
10. Imagine 93
11. A Promise 103

SECTION 3: PROMISES

12. What He Said 115

13. Sing to It 125

14. Sing in Faith 135

15. He's Got You 145

16. It's Time 155

Introduction

Your Bible is filled with dreamers. Have you ever noticed that? I'm not just talking about dreamers of the kind of dreams you have while sleeping. Although there are many of those in the Bible, too, including Jacob, Joseph, Solomon, and Daniel.

No, I'm talking about dreamers of the kinds of dreams God puts in the hearts of His children — dreams of *being* things, *doing* things, *building* things, or *accomplishing* things. These God-dreams always seem too big, too grand, or too lofty to ever be reachable. But that's how you know a dream is from God. If you can conceive of a way to achieve it in your own power, it's probably not from God!

These dreams are powerful indicators of what God actually created you to be and do in this life. His plan is for you to be significant. His dreams for you are good and glorious.

Yet life has a way of trying to crush those kinds of dreams, doesn't it? Setbacks and opposition can cause discouragement. And it's easy for discouragement to lead to despair. For far too many of God's children, the dream He gave them long ago has gotten buried.

Too many have simply stopped dreaming. Maybe that's you. That's why I've written this short book. Its message is a simple one.

It's time to dream again. Let's get started.

SECTION 1:
Dreams

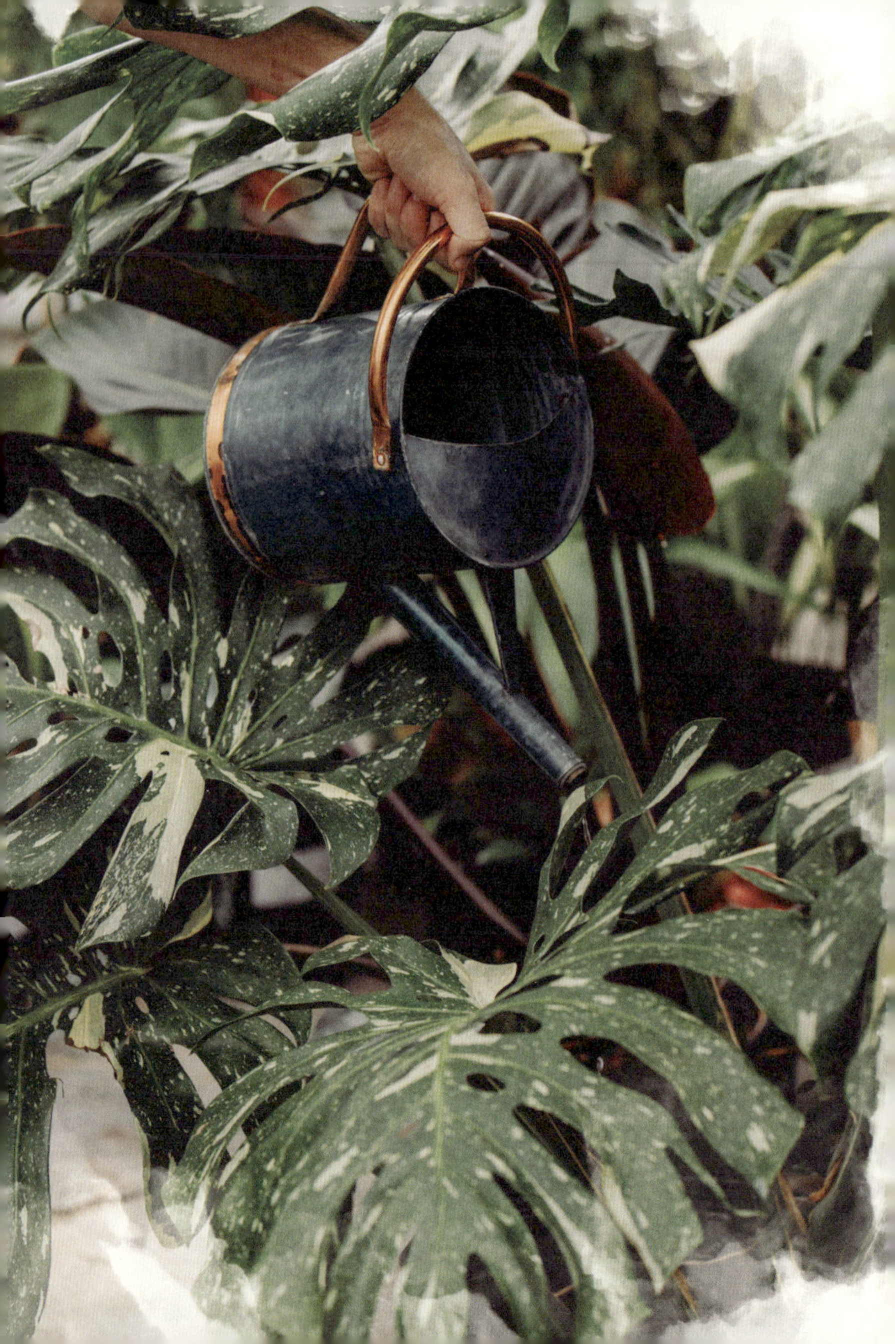

CHAPTER 1
Buried Dreams

You watched me as I was being formed in utter seclusion, as I was woven together in the dark of the womb. You saw me before I was born. Every day of my life was recorded in your book. Every moment was laid out before a single day had passed.

PSALM 139:15-16 (NLT)

God Dreamed About You

Here's an amazing thought: *God has dreams for you.* It's true!

Have you ever considered the dreams your Heavenly Father has for you? God has high hopes for your life. Long before your birth, He envisioned and crafted you, designing you to fulfill the dream He has for your life.

Within each of us, there are dreams that line up with God's good designs and plans for us. In other words, these dreams align with how He uniquely fashioned us. There are things we are fervently believing for and goals we are striving to achieve — dreams instilled in us by God, our Creator, that correspond with our unique design.

God had you in mind — a carefully crafted design — before bringing you into being. In other words, you carry a purposeful design. As God declared to Jeremiah, *"Before I formed you in the womb I knew you, before you were born I set you apart; I appointed you as a prophet to the nations"* (Jeremiah 1:5, NIV).

The idea that God affectionately and purposefully designed each of our lives uniquely is hard to imagine. It reveals the magnificence of God's nature and the depth of His love for you. Think about this: He, who is infinite, all-knowing, all-powerful, and omnipresent, dreamed of you and carefully fashioned every detail of your life to fulfill a dream.

Pause and think about this: You were in God's heart and mind before He shaped and formed you. He cares deeply about the details of your life, designing all of your days. Consider God doing this for billions of people throughout human history, and then realize that He did it specifically for you and me — truly amazing.

Your Destiny

Dreams are keys to your destiny. They are one of the ways God gently guides you toward a glorious future. The Bible says that your Heavenly Father has plans, a design, for your life. Psalm 138:8 (NLT) declares, *The LORD will work out his plans for my life.*

God uniquely made you and planted His desires within you — desires that manifest as your dreams. These dreams are a divine gift from God, referred to in Scripture as the secret petitions of our hearts —

perhaps aspirations you haven't shared with anyone. The Bible reminds us, *Delight yourself in the LORD, and He will give you the desires and petitions of your heart* (Psalm 37:4, AMP).

As a child, you might have dreamt of being someone special, of doing something that brings joy to your heart when you think about it. Those dreams might very well be an indicator of your purpose and destiny. God promised to fulfill those desires or dreams as we trust and obey.

Buried Dreams

Sure, setbacks come our way. Maybe you got passed over for that promotion. Maybe a desired relationship didn't materialize. Or perhaps you walked away from a visit to the doctor's office with discouraging news. Life tends to suppress our dreams, burying them under discouragement and past mistakes. Some dreams may seem to have died, buried beneath rejection, divorce, failure, or negative voices. It's easy to settle for a less-than life when the dream has been buried. And when a dream is buried, it's easily forgotten.

God promised to fulfill those desires or
dreams as we trust and obey.

JOEL OSTEEN

But here's wonderful news: Just because you gave up on your dream doesn't mean God gave up on it. Remember, it's His dream, too.

Your dream may be buried, but the good news is that it's still alive. It lives within you. Here's even better news: It's not too late to see it come to pass. Stop saying, "It's never going happen," "I'm never going to have a nice house," "I'm never going to get married," or whatever your dream might be. Instead say, "I'm surrounded by God's favor. Blessings are chasing me down. He's placed His dreams in my heart, and I am stepping into them!"

Remove the Dirt

Instead of giving into thoughts like, *It will never happen,* which only adds more dirt and buries the dream deeper, why not grab a shovel and start clearing away the dirt? Express gratitude to the Lord, saying, "Thank You for restoring health to me. I am free from this addiction, free from this depression. Thank You that my best days lie ahead." By maintaining positive thoughts and declarations, the buried dream is unearthed, bit by bit.

Delight yourself in the LORD, and He will give you the desires and petitions of your heart.

PSALM 37:4 (AMP)

Delight yourself in
the LORD, and He
will give you the
desires and petitions
of your heart.

PSALM 37:4 (AMP)

Choosing a more positive mindset and putting hope-filled words in your mouth opens the door for God to work wonders. He responds to our faith — not our doubts, discouragement, or complaints — as He intimately knows the truth about our destiny and purpose. Collaborate with Him to see it come to fulfillment.

Having thoughts like, *I could never achieve my goal, I'll never get this promotion, I lack the talent,* and *I always get passed over,* which only further bury the dream, means it's time to get a shovel and unearth that dream. For some, it might require heavy equipment, as it's buried deep. Dig it up, breathe life into it. It all begins in your thoughts, beliefs, and expressions.

God entrusted you with the dream, completing His part. Now it's your turn to stir up your faith and believe in the dream He placed within you. The Enemy seeks to keep your dream buried and tries to convince you it will never happen, that it's too late. Reject those lies; he is a deceiver and the Father of Lies (John 8:44).

You can still achieve your dreams, become all God created you to be, and fulfill your destiny. Each time you recall your dream and express gratitude to the Lord for bringing it to pass, you're removing some dirt, excavating, and bringing it closer to realization.

Declaration Prayer of Destiny

Heavenly Father,

I declare that You, in Your infinite love, designed me with a purpose before my birth. I embrace the idea that my dreams align with Your divine plan for my life. I affirm that You never give up on Your promises.

I declare that my destiny is intertwined with my dreams, which are Your way of guiding me. I recognize the unique design and desires You have placed within me. I commit to unearthing and nurturing the dreams buried by life's challenges, knowing that they are still alive and part of Your plan for my destiny.

I declare that the key to reaching my destiny is in remembering my dreams and trusting in Your promises. Despite disappointments and doubts, I choose to focus on the dreams You placed in my heart. I believe that it's never too late, and with Your support, I will see Your dream for me fulfilled.

I declare gratitude for Your deep love, care, and purpose for my life. I accept Your creative design, commit to holding tightly to my dreams, and declare that my destiny will unfold according to Your perfect plan.

In Jesus' name, amen.

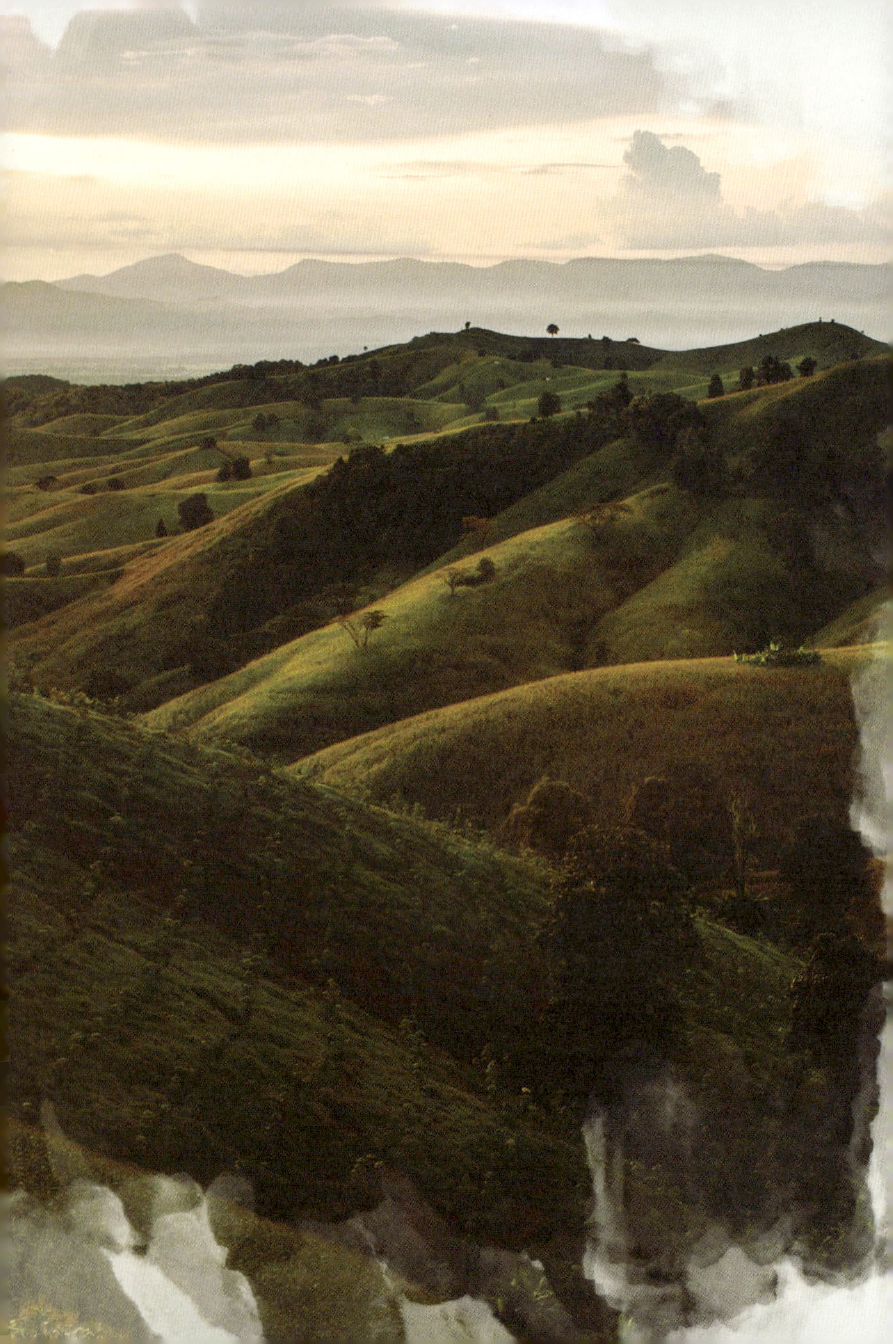

CHAPTER 2

Remember

"So now, give me this hill country about which the LORD spoke that day, for you heard on that day that the [giant-like] Anakim were there, with great fortified cities; perhaps the LORD will be with me, and I shall drive them out just as the LORD said."

JOSHUA 14:12 (AMP)

The Starting Point

Has it been a while since you embraced or even thought of your dreams? This is an important question because the key to reaching your destiny is remembering your dream. Recall what God promised you. Remember the whispers in the middle of the night, the dreams placed within you during childhood or young adulthood, back when anything and everything seemed possible.

Somewhere along the line, disappointments, setbacks, criticisms, and other life challenges can cause us to forget those dreams. You might think it's too late, too big, or simply impossible. You may doubt your ability to write that book, start that business, mend that relationship, or complete that degree.

Instead of dwelling on the hurt, the failures, and the times it didn't work out, reverse the narrative. Start remembering your dream. Remember that lofty goal you once held. Rekindle your passion. You haven't missed your opportunity. You haven't had too many setbacks. You are not lacking, and you haven't been shortchanged. God will support you to see His dream for you fulfilled.

As long as you hold onto disappointment and discouragement, you'll remain stuck. Begin to recall the dream: "Lord, You put that vision in my heart. So, I thank You for divine connections and open doors and abundant favor!"

What did God place in your heart long ago? What used to ignite your excitement? It is time to dream again.

Believe Again

It may seem impossible. Maybe all the voices around you say it's not going to happen. You've pushed it down and buried it in your past. Perhaps you are even afraid to mention it to anyone because you assume they will laugh at the idea. God is saying, "I'm still going to do what I've promised you. I spoke it, I put it in your heart. It may not have happened yet, but I am true to My word. It's on the way."

If you'll start believing again, get your passion back, and stir your faith up, God can resurrect what you thought was dead. Dreams you've given up on, dreams you tried and failed, are suddenly going to come back to life. Problems that look permanent are going to suddenly turn around. What should have taken years God is going to do in a fraction of the time. He has the final say. He hasn't changed His mind.

Divine Detours

Refuse to be defeated by circumstances or let go of your dream. Even when you can't comprehend the reasons behind challenges — a person leaving, illness striking, or a business failing — remember that it's part of a divine process. Every unfair situation, delay, and closed door isn't just a setback; it's a setup for God to guide you to where He intends you to be. Though the journey may seem prolonged, and the path unclear, a touch of God's favor can change everything.

Recognize that God is not solely focused on the fulfillment of your dream but is equally invested in your personal growth. His interest lies not just in achieving goals but in shaping your character. God desires you to become the best version of yourself and will ensure you are equipped to fulfill the destiny He has laid out for you.

Though the journey may seem prolonged, and the path unclear, a touch of God's favor can change everything.

JOEL OSTEEN

What appears as a detour is a vital part of your development. God understands that delays, trials, obstacles, and even attacks from the Enemy contribute to your growth. As the Bible wisely advises, *When troubles of any kind come your way, consider it an opportunity for great joy . . . when your faith is tested, your endurance has a chance to grow. So let it grow, for when your endurance is fully developed, you will be perfect and complete, needing nothing* (James 1:2–4, NLT). Embrace challenges as opportunities for joy, knowing they contribute to your spiritual maturity.

Caleb

Caleb and Joshua, as young men, spied out the Promised Land and believed they could conquer it. Despite Caleb and Joshua's confidence, most of the spies succumbed to fear, preventing the Israelites from entering. Caleb, though discouraged, refused to let his dream die. Many gave up, but Caleb, a true champion, shook off the dirt thrown on his dream and remained resilient. God said of him, *"My servant Caleb, because he has a different spirit in him and has followed Me fully, I will bring into the land where he went, and his descendants shall inherit it"* (Numbers 14:24, NKJV).

Forty years later, at eighty-five years old, Caleb revisited the same mountain and declared, "God, give me this mountain," despite its challenges. There were formidable giants on that mountain, but Caleb chose to fight for the promise over ease. Despite setbacks and age, he conquered the mountain, and realized the dream burning within him.

"So now, give me this hill country about which the LORD spoke that day, for you heard on that day that the [giant-like] Anakim were there, with great fortified cities; perhaps the LORD will be with me, and I shall drive them out just as the LORD said" (Joshua 14:12, AMP).

Have your dreams been buried? Maybe you once aspired to achieve greatness but faced setbacks. Despite the challenges, like Caleb, don't settle. Try again and stir up those dreams, shake off the excuses, and pursue the mountains that God has placed in your heart. Even if it takes time, your dreams can come to pass.

Try Again

Regardless of past attempts — whether it was a year, five years, or forty years ago — if your dream didn't materialize and no one supported or encouraged you, know that the dream is still alive. God echoes to you what He told Caleb: "Go back and try again. This is your moment; your destiny is calling out to you."

Like Caleb, refuse to adopt a spirit of giving up or choosing the easy path. Don't settle for less; your destiny is at stake. Instead of saying, "I'm content with less, I don't want the struggle," recognize that stirring up your gifts is essential. Missing your created purpose is at risk. The fulfillment of your dream brings immense joy, and settling for anything less than God's intention for you won't satisfy.

Even if you've faced setbacks, rise again and declare, "God, give me that same mountain. I won't settle for substitutes, second best, or less than what You put in my heart." When you recall the dream, God can empower you to achieve what eluded you before. Your journey to becoming all you were created to be is still within reach.

Declaration Prayer to Remember

Heavenly Father,

Regardless of past setbacks and a lack of support, I remember the dream You gave me and declare that my dormant dream remains alive. Like Caleb, I choose not to succumb to a spirit of giving up or settling for an easy path. Your destiny for me is at stake, and I commit to stirring up the gifts You've given me and understanding that settling for less than Your intention is not an option.

I reject substitutes, second best, and anything less than what You have placed in my heart. As I recall the dream, I confidently believe that You will empower me to achieve what eluded me before. The journey to realizing my created purpose and becoming everything I was meant to be is still within my grasp, and I embrace this fresh start with determination and faith.

In Jesus' name, amen.

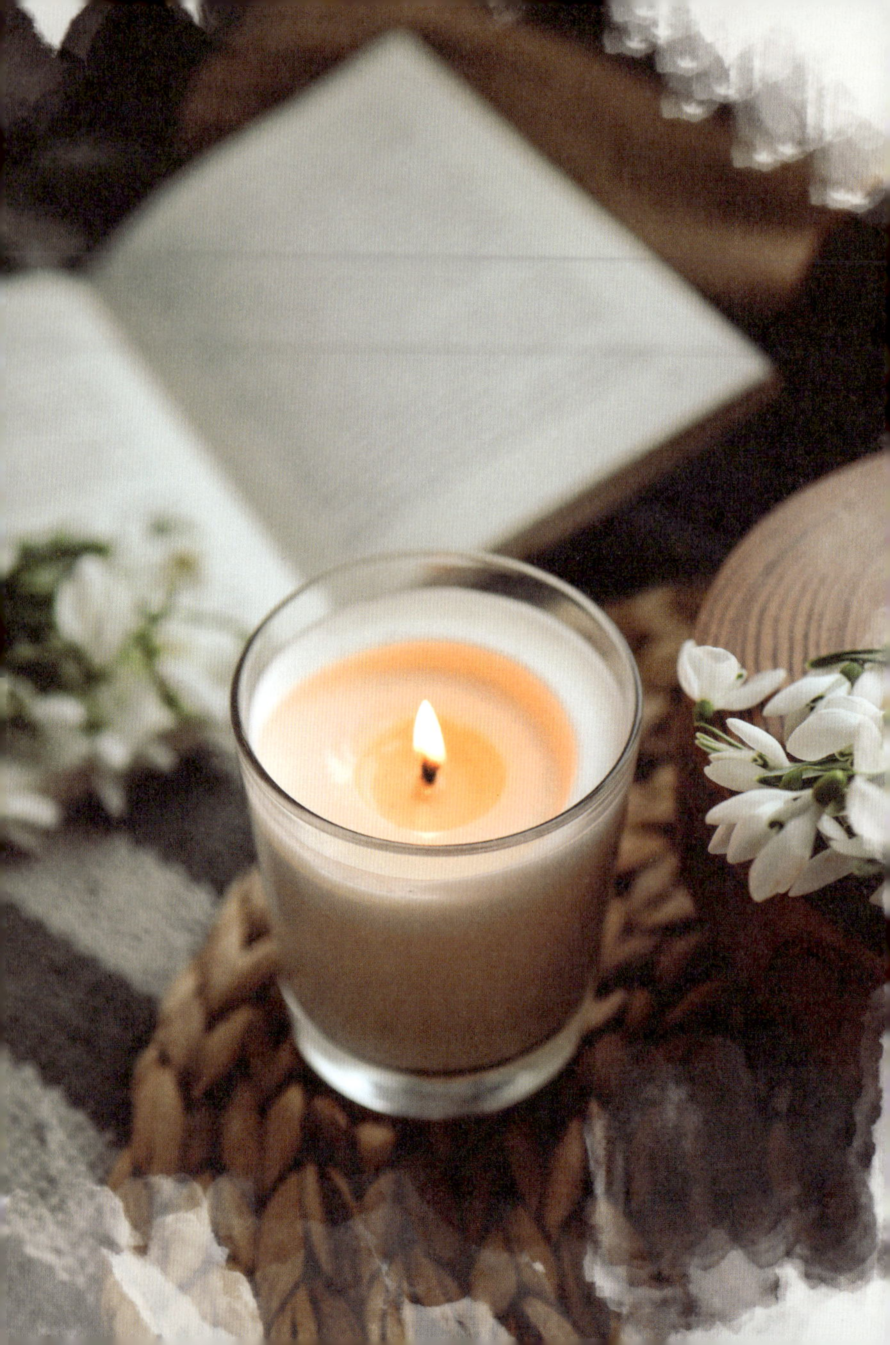

CHAPTER 3

Light the Fire

At Gibeon the LORD appeared to Solomon in a dream by night; and God said, "Ask! What shall I give you?"

1 KINGS 3:5 (NKJV)

It's There

When God breathed His life into you, He equipped you with everything needed to fulfill your destiny. No person, setback, disappointment, or loss can hinder you. Why? Because the Most High God is with you. Royal blood flows through your veins, and seeds of greatness reside within you!

There are dreams in you so big that you can't accomplish them on your own. In fact, that's how you know they are God-given. If you can do it on your own, it's probably not a God-dream. God-dreams can only come to pass through your connection to your Heavenly Father.

But they also require faith — a firm belief in your destiny — and trust that God is guiding your steps. Trust that, despite challenges, every circumstance is orchestrated to bring forth good in your life.

Look again at this key scripture: *At Gibeon the* Lord *appeared to Solomon in a dream by night; and God said, "Ask! What shall I give you?"* (1 Kings 3:5, NKJV).

If you've been grappling with delayed dreams, don't quit. Your purpose and destiny may feel buried, but they are alive within you. Reignite your faith,

At Gibeon, the LORD appeared to Solomon in a dream by night; and God said, "Ask! What shall I give you?"

1 KINGS 3:5 (NKJV)

At Gibeon, the
LORD appeared to
Solomon in a dream
by night; and God
said, "Ask! What shall
I give you?"

1 KINGS 3:5 (NKJV)

continue to trust, and God can bring them to pass. The dream is still there.

Ignite the Flame

What you once gave up on, God never abandoned. The dreams you harbored earlier in life persist within you. Jeremiah 20:9 (NLT) describes it this way: *His word burns in my heart like a fire. It's like a fire in my bones!* Your destiny is calling, and despite past setbacks — missed opportunities and unfavorable reports — know that this is a new day.

God initiated this journey, and He will see it through to completion. Missed opportunities and lost time can be restored. Even if circumstances or choices have led to setbacks, God knows how to make up for lost years. Embrace the promise of another chance, confident that God can still lead you to where you are meant to be.

Joseph's Dream

As a young man, Joseph received a dream from God that envisioned his future rule over a nation. Unfortunately, he shared the part about his brothers bowing down before him, which proved unwise. Some dreams are best kept to oneself; not everyone can handle what God has placed inside you. Instead of celebrating, some people may become jealous and critical.

When Joseph visited his brothers, their sarcastic response when they saw him coming was, *"Here comes the dreamer"* (Genesis 37:19, NLT). Their discontent stemmed from his determination to break free, achieve greatness, and make a lasting impact. Joseph's brothers would have accepted him if he settled for mediocrity, but his belief in the seeds of greatness within him unsettled them. When you stir up the gifts God placed within you and believe in your potential for greatness, be prepared — not everyone will celebrate your journey.

Overcome the Critics

When pursuing your dreams, expect detractors. Jealous folks may attempt to undermine you. The envious or bitter may try to discourage you. Whether it's whispered doubts about your abilities or subtle comments on your age or past experiences, let such

When pursuing your dreams,
expect detractors.

JOEL OSTEEN

negativity pass right through without taking root in your heart.

Critics, naysayers, and haters don't dictate your destiny; God does. Despite their efforts to slow you down or shut you down, God can turn their actions around for your promotion. Just like Joseph's brothers tried to suppress his dream, sometimes even close relatives may not celebrate your journey. Don't waste energy on battles that don't matter, trying to prove yourself to them. You don't need their approval; you have God's approval. Don't let their negativity distract you. Keep moving forward, pursuing your destiny, and let God handle the rest. Successful people focus on what God has placed in their hearts, not on what others are doing or saying.

Unleash the Dreamer Within

You wouldn't have that opposition if you didn't have something great in you. If your dream weren't alive and on track, you wouldn't encounter such challenges. The Enemy recognizes a dreamer in you — a person full of faith, embracing the belief in seeds of greatness and undeterred by circumstances or setbacks. As a dreamer, you understand the favor of God, believing in the possibility of the impossible, and knowing that all things work together for your good.

Being a dreamer makes you a formidable force against the Enemy. You are signaling your ascent to new levels and your determination to set higher standards for your family. The Enemy knows you're destined for abundance and overflow, and he is powerless to stop you. Though he may attempt to convince you to settle, remember that negative circumstances are not halting your destiny; they are indicators that you are on the path to it. Every setback, every wrong done to you, every moment it didn't work out is merely another step toward your ultimate destiny.

Fulfillment of a Dream

Joseph's journey was marked by betrayal and hardship. From being thrown into a pit by jealous brothers to enduring slavery and imprisonment, it seemed his dream of ruling a nation was slipping away. Falsely accused by Potiphar's wife, Joseph found himself in prison for years. Even promises from fellow inmates brought disappointment. However, Joseph kept a good attitude despite everything happening to him. One day Joseph's interpretation of Pharaoh's dream changed everything. Elevated to a position of authority, Joseph became a key figure during a severe famine.

Years later, Joseph faced the very brothers who had caused him so much pain. Instead of bitterness, anger, or revenge, the scripture says, when Joseph saw his brothers, *He remembered the dreams he'd had about them many years before* (Genesis 42:9, NLT). Amidst the hurt and betrayal, he held onto the promise God had spoken to him. Joseph's seemingly missed destiny and series of bad breaks were part of God's plan to lead him to where he was meant to be. God took what appeared harmful and turned it around for Joseph's ultimate good, and He can for you too. Ignite the flame inside you to pursue the dream God gave you despite the opposition.

Declaration Prayer of Passion

Heavenly Father,

I trust in the journey You have set in motion and am confident You will bring it to pass. Despite missed opportunities and lost time, I believe in Your power to restore and redeem.

I commit to staying focused on Your plan and not allowing negativity to derail me. With unwavering faith, I acknowledge the seeds of greatness within me and remain resilient in the face of challenges and setbacks.

You've molded me into a dreamer, aware of Your favor, believing in the potential of the impossible. I am steadfast in the knowledge that all circumstances work together for my ultimate good.

In Jesus' name, amen.

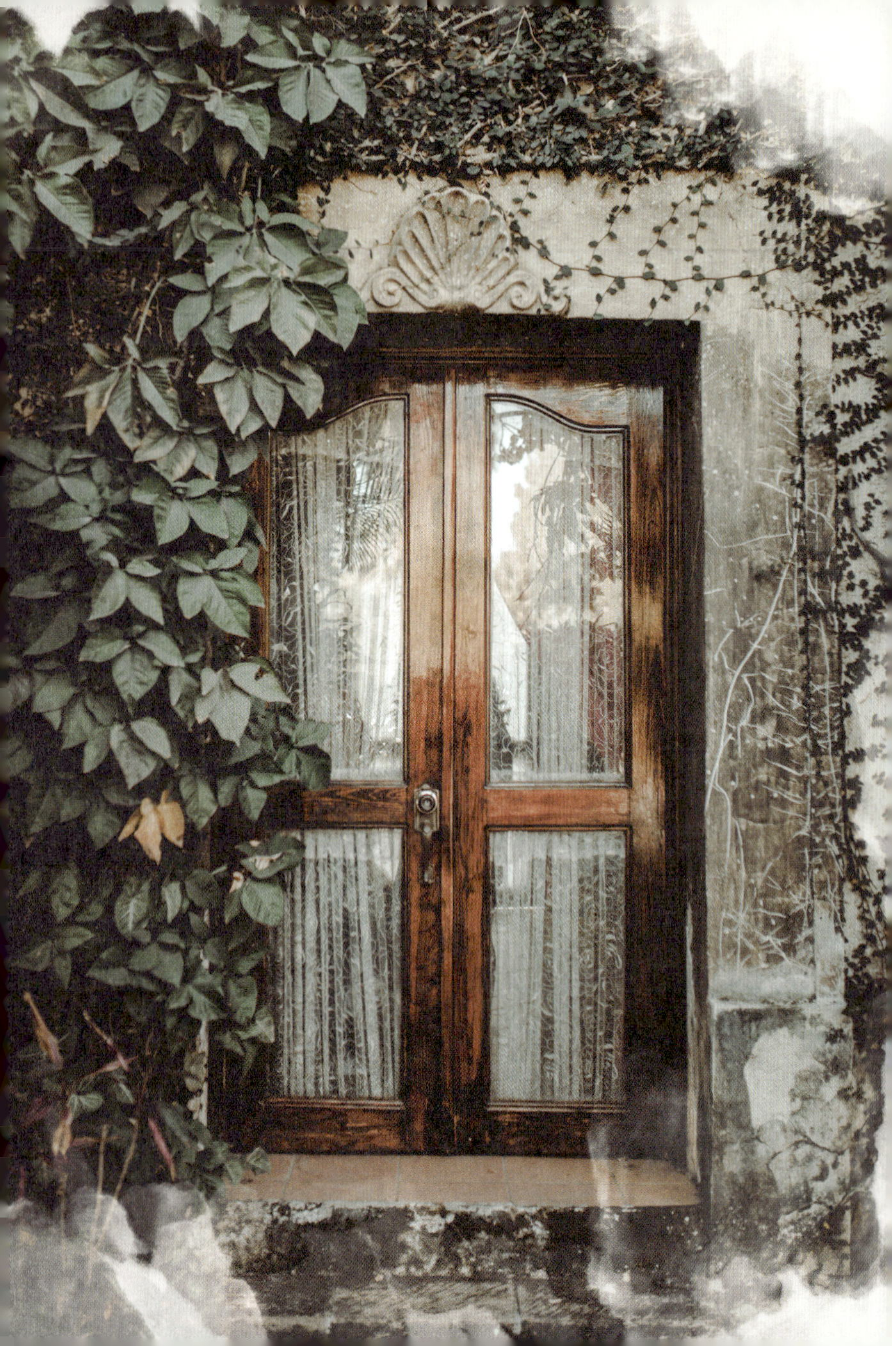

CHAPTER 4
Dream Big

*"Ask, and it will be given to you;
seek, and you will find; knock, and it
will be opened to you."*

MATTHEW 7:7 (NKJV)

God's Dream

God's dream for your life is so much bigger than your own. He wants to do extraordinary things in you, through you, and with you. If you're going to see God's dream for your life fulfilled, you must learn to pray bold prayers and make faith-filled declarations about that dream.

Often, believers hesitate to ask for too much, fearing they are being greedy or selfish. I have people tell me, "Joel, if God wants me to be blessed, He'll bless me. He's God." But that is not the way it works. God expects us to ask Him. The Scripture says, *You do not have because you do not ask* (James 4:2, NKJV). Maying big requests doesn't annoy God; it delights Him. He likes it when you ask big things. So, pray for His favor, blessings, and increase at levels far beyond what seems possible. With God all things are possible (Matthew 19:26)!

Big Prayers

At times, many believers find themselves praying small prayers like, "God, if You'll just help my marriage survive, I'd be happy," or "If You'll just help

He likes it when you ask big things. So, pray for His favor, blessings, and increase at levels far beyond what seems possible.

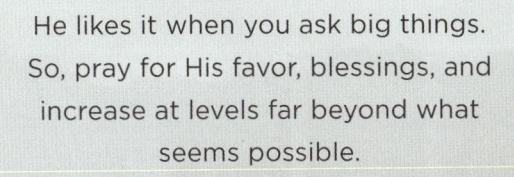

JOEL OSTEEN

me make ends meet this month." Some think only to pray, "Lord, help my children stay in school." These prayers are too low. As people of faith, it's essential to be more daring, to aim higher. Stretch your faith and pray for a thriving marriage relationship, abundant provision with overflow to bless others, and children who are diligent and excelling.

Declare, "Father, You said my children would be mighty in the land, so I'm asking that they prosper, become leaders, and fulfill their God-given destinies."

Jesus put it this way: *"According to your faith be it done to you"* (Matthew 9:29, ESV). What Jesus was saying is according to your trust, confidence, and belief in My power and My ability it will be done to you. Essentially, if you pray with little faith, you'll receive little. But if you learn to pray big, bold prayers, expecting and believing in God's power and ability, it opens the door for Him to do significant things in your life.

Ask Big

You might have a dream deep within that you've never spoken to God about. While you should pray for others, it's also essential to start asking God for what He has placed in your heart. Asking is not wrong or selfish; in fact, Scripture encourages it. Psalm 2:8 (NKJV) declares, *"Ask of Me, and I will give You the nations for Your inheritance, and the ends of the earth for Your possession."*

God invites you to request big things, including those hidden dreams He planted in your heart and unborn promises that may seem unattainable. In your quiet moments with God, dare to ask for your deepest hopes and dreams even if they appear impossible. Be honest, saying, "God, I don't see how this could ever happen, but I dream of starting my own business. I'm asking for Your help." Or, "God, I'd love to return to college, but I lack the time and money. I'm asking You to make a way." Dare to seek God for your greatest dreams and desires.

Debt Forgiven

I once spoke with a woman whose prematurely born child spent more than a year in the hospital, accumulating overwhelming medical bills that exceeded $3 million. Facing a lifetime of repayment on a schoolteacher's income, she received an unexpected letter from the hospital. The board had decided to forgive her debt in full and returned the past payments she had made.

Imagine if she had prayed for merely enough to cover monthly payments before receiving the letter. God's intention was to bless her by forgiving the debt entirely. This story encourages us to make big requests of God and dream big. Trust that God can accomplish the impossible, even when it seems implausible. Believe in His unique plan for you that will unfold unexpectedly and extraordinarily.

Believe Big

Dreams that seem so big and distant are closer than you think. Anticipate everything falling into place, unexpected promotions finding you, and promises being fulfilled. You are reading this because God is about to do something extraordinary, something beyond your current understanding. Don't talk yourself out of it — simply believe.

I ask you today: Are you ready to believe and stretch your faith? Will you dare to believe big and

Believe in His unique plan for you that will unfold unexpectedly and extraordinarily.

JOEL OSTEEN

ask big? Praying half-hearted prayers may cause you to miss out on God's best for you. Understand that the God who breathed life into you, set you apart, and crowned you with favor is more than enough. He has big dreams for you. Will you dream big with Him?

Declaration Prayer of Big Dreams

Heavenly Father,

In gratitude, I come before You and recognize Your dream for my life exceeds my own. I embrace the power of bold prayers, understanding Your expectation that I approach with big requests — for favor, blessings, and extraordinary increase. Help me break free from small requests and instill in me the courage to pray for substantial blessings, unlocking the door for Your significant work in my life.

As the Bible declares, *"According to your faith be it done to you"* (Matthew 9:29, ESV). I choose to embrace bold, big prayers and trust in Your unmatched power. Lord, I bring before You my desires, including hidden dreams and seemingly unattainable promises. Open my eyes of faith to anticipate unexpected outcomes, fulfilled promises, and extraordinary results.

In this moment, I sense Your presence and a divine invitation to believe big and ask big. I understand that You, the God who breathed life into me, have big dreams for me. I align my dreams with Yours and trust You to lead me into extraordinary fulfillment.

In Jesus' name, amen.

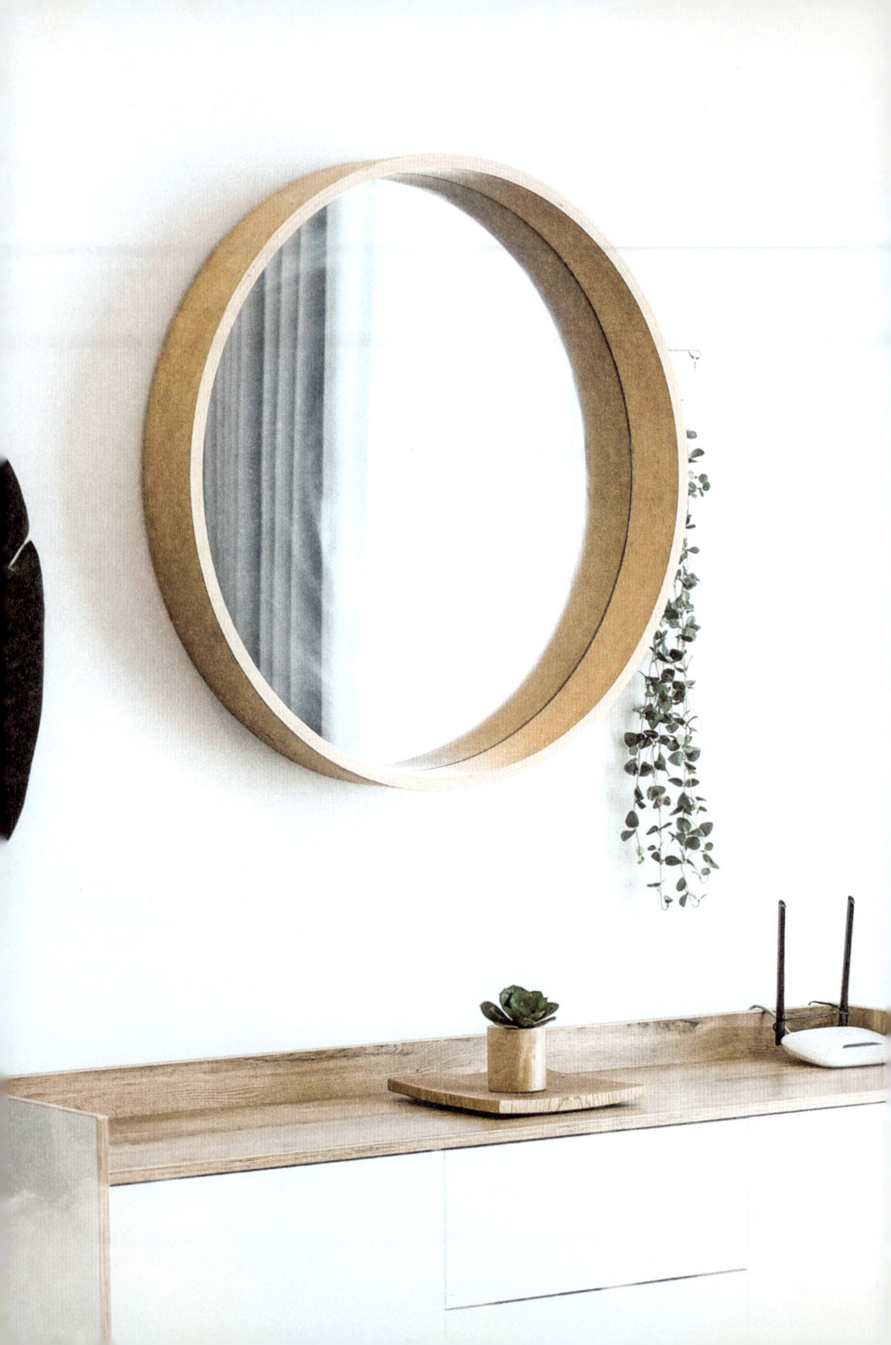

CHAPTER 5
Hidden Treasure

Now to Him who is able to [carry out His purpose and] do superabundantly more than all that we dare ask or think [infinitely beyond our greatest prayers, hopes, or dreams], according to His power that is at work within us.

EPHESIANS 3:20 (AMP)

Discovering the Treasure

Have you ever felt confined, fenced in, or stuck in life? When that happens, it's easy to believe you've reached your limits. Thoughts like *I can't go any further, my dreams are out of reach,* or *it's too late for me* can be discouraging — or even depressing. Please know that those are lies.

Here's the truth. If God has planted a dream in you, He has also equipped you with the ability to fulfill it — with His help. The challenge often lies in understanding that your God-given dream is like hidden treasure within you. It's in there, just waiting to be discovered.

Deep within you are unexplored gifts and talents with untapped potential awaiting release to propel you toward your dreams. God, in His intricate plan for your life, deposited within you the skills, wisdom, creativity — everything essential for your destiny.

But hidden treasure that remains hidden doesn't benefit anyone. It's not just what you *possess* but what you *bring out*. To reach your utmost potential, you must access that concealed treasure.

The continent of Africa reportedly holds more natural resources of gold, diamonds, and oil than any other, surpassing North America, Europe, and Asia. Yet, Africa faces challenges and economic struggles because these treasures are hidden and often unknown or inaccessible to the local people.

Within you lies hidden treasure in the form of God-given resources, ideas, or strategies. It might be books, movies, songs, ideas, inventions, businesses — all placed there by the Creator to be discovered by you. What a tragedy to carry this treasure to the grave undiscovered or unused.

Being Yourself

You have something to offer this world that nobody else can. You are one of a kind. In fact, you are uniquely anointed and equipped to achieve the dream God put inside you. Avoid the trap of yearning for someone else's gift. Having their gift wouldn't benefit you; it would hinder you. You aren't meant to replicate others but to be yourself.

God deliberately crafted you with specific traits, a distinct personality, and capabilities that fit your unique purpose. You are intellectually and artistically capable, possessing precisely what you need to fulfill your dream. Don't overlook the treasure waiting to be unveiled — your authentic self, fully equipped and ready to make a profound impact.

You've been fearfully and wonderfully crafted as a one-of-a-kind individual. There's no need to compare yourself to others; for when we measure ourselves against others the Bible calls it unwise (2 Corinthians 10:12). As you confidently walk in your anointing, fully aware of the incredible and unique creation God designed you to be, your hidden treasure, gifts, and untapped potential will be released, propelling you into the fullness of your destiny.

His Power

Ephesians 3:20 (AMP) says, *Now to Him who is able to* [*carry out His purpose and*] *do superabundantly more than all that we dare ask or think* [*infinitely beyond our greatest prayers, hopes, or dreams*], *according to **His power that is at work within us.*** That last part is the key. Notice it's not according to the power that's in your neighbor, your boss, your pastor, your priest,

As you confidently walk in your anointing, fully aware of the incredible and unique creation God designed you to be, your hidden treasure, gifts, and untapped potential will be released, propelling you into the fullness of your destiny.

JOEL OSTEEN

the bank, or the stock market. It's according to God's power that works in you.

You carry a treasure, the resources, and God's power to fulfill your destiny. To unveil it, embrace the attitude that says, *I've got what it takes. The treasure is already deposited in me — I am equipped, empowered, talented, creative, and well-able.* Living with this mindset will open your eyes to the exceeding greatness of God's favor in your life.

The Promise in You

Consider the story of Sarah, Abraham's wife, who nearly missed the fulfillment of God's promise. Despite her age, God assured her of a child (Genesis 18:10–12). Sarah, however, initially doubted that the treasure was within her and took matters into her own hands. She thought the promise would come through somebody else since she was too old to have a child, which made sense to her natural mind. So, she got her husband, Abraham, together with a young maid named Hagar, and they had a baby.

When God reminded Sarah that the promise wasn't in someone else but in her, He was essentially saying, "You have hidden treasure still buried in your womb." However, because Sarah entertained thoughts like *I'm too old* and *I'm at a disadvantage*, she remained distant from God's best.

Then at almost 100 years old, Sarah birthed a baby boy named Isaac, and the treasure within her was finally revealed. It didn't come through somebody else or rely on the power of her maid or husband. Sarah chose to believe God's promise and saw His power firsthand. Sensing the treasure inside her, she declared, "This is my time, my destiny. There's something stirring within me — potential, dreams, gifts, promises waiting to be released."

Learn from Sarah's triumph over doubts and misconceptions. Acknowledge that God has deposited His promises and hidden treasures within you. Don't talk yourself out of the extraordinary things God wants to accomplish through you by underestimating your worth or the potential of your treasure. You are not too old, disadvantaged, or lacking — God's promise is in you.

Place a Demand

When I was a little boy, our neighbors had a big German shepherd dog. Despite their fenced yard, they usually kept the dog on a leash. One day, while I was playing baseball with some friends, the ball went into their yard. Without much thought, I got a ladder and climbed over our six-foot fence to retrieve it. To my surprise, the dog charged toward me at full speed. For some reason, he was not on a leash that day.

Panic set in; I thought I was going to die. I sprinted back to my fence, praying for forgiveness. When I got to the fence, all in one motion, I grabbed it with one hand and jumped as high as I could, and somehow, I cleared the fence right before the dog got to me. I was just a little boy. I had practically jumped over a six-foot fence. In that moment, I discovered untapped potential and unearthed hidden treasure within myself.

That dog helped me unearth potential I wasn't aware of and discover hidden treasure within myself. You won't truly grasp what's inside until you place a demand on your potential.

Declaration Prayer of Hidden Treasure

Heavenly Father,

I gratefully acknowledge the unique treasure within me, planted by Your divine hand. Grant me wisdom to recognize and courage to unveil the gifts and talents You've intricately placed in me. Guide me to tap into the rich resources hidden within rather than allowing them to lie dormant.

I acknowledge that Your power works within me, and You've given me what it takes. The treasure is already deposited in me — I am equipped, empowered, talented, creative, and well-able with Your power at work to fulfill my dreamed destiny.

I declare that I will not go through life with the treasure still buried within me. Empower me to unearth the unique contributions You've planted in my being and awaken the destiny You have purposed for me.

In Jesus' name, amen.

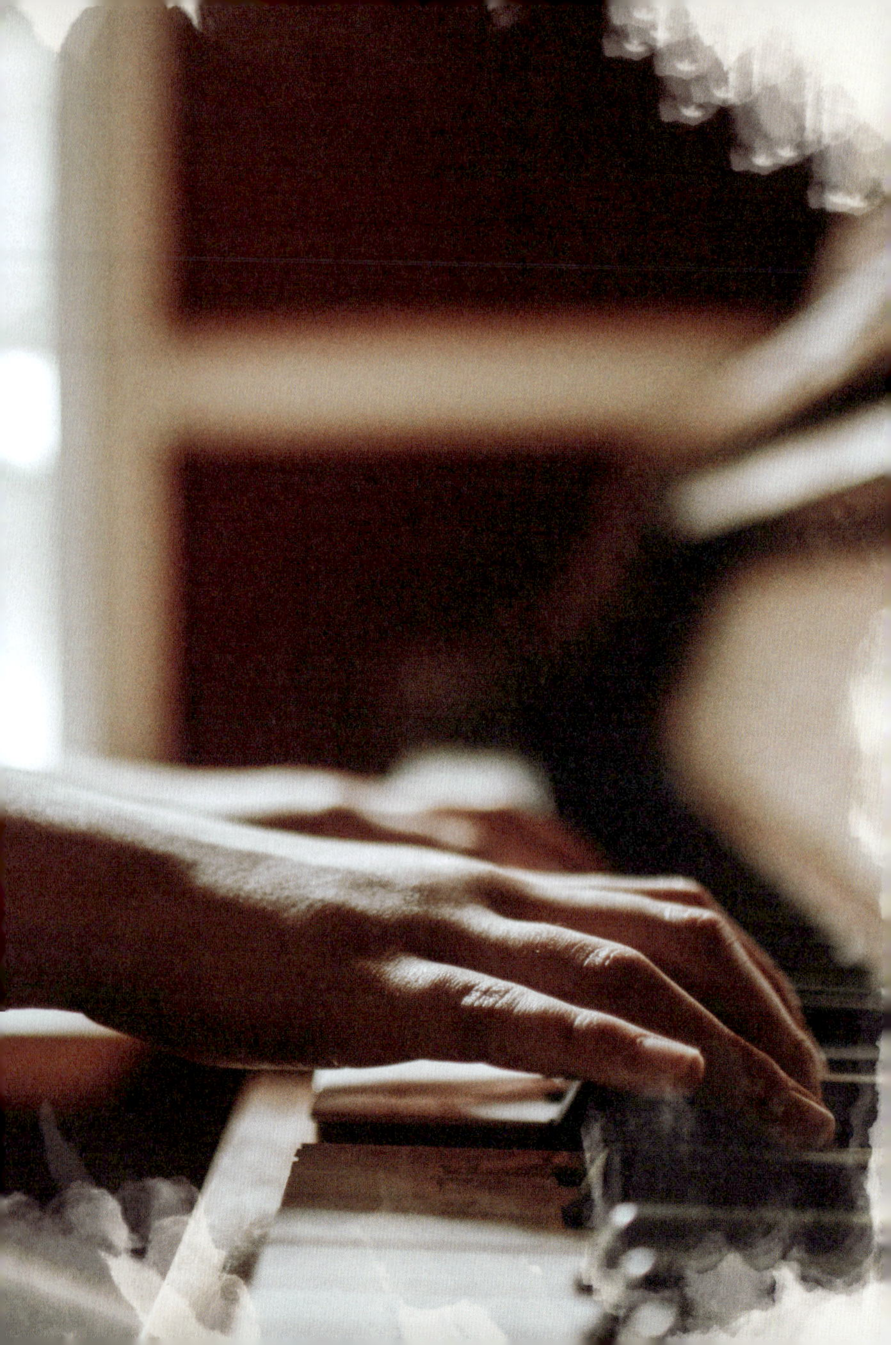

CHAPTER 6
The Master

For we are his workmanship, created in Christ Jesus for good works, which God prepared beforehand, that we should walk in them.

EPHESIANS 2:10 (ESV)

Chopsticks

I read a story about a five-year-old boy who was deeply passionate about the piano. Every chance that he got, he played. He never had any formal lessons or any kind of training. In fact, some people told him he was too young and too small to ever be great. But despite those comments he continued practicing day after day. The only song he really knew how to play was the very simple tune called "Chopsticks."

One day his father surprised him with tickets to the symphony featuring a world-renowned Italian pianist. This man was one of the greatest piano players in the world. That night, on the way to their seats, the little boy noticed the beautiful grand piano up on the stage. When no one was watching he quietly slipped over and sat down and began to play his elementary version of "Chopsticks."

About that time the curtain began to rise. Everyone was expecting to see the world-renowned pianist. Instead, they saw this little five-year-old boy. He was so caught up with his playing he didn't realize what was happening. When he finally looked up, he froze in fear.

When the Master steps in, He mixes His excellence with your average and amazing things will begin to happen.

JOEL OSTEEN

He Stepped In

Just as he was about to bolt toward his seat, he felt two big arms reach around him. To his surprise it was the world-renowned pianist. He whispered in the little boy's ears, "Keep playing." The boy continued playing that elementary version of "Chopsticks." This world-renowned piano player started playing a piece of a Beethoven symphony that was scored in the same cadence and the same key. Under the direction of the master, he nodded to the rest of the orchestra. First bringing in the woodwinds, then the percussion, then the brass.

The father sat there in the audience overwhelmed by what he witnessed. He never dreamed that simple tune he had heard so many times would no longer sound like "Chopsticks" and would become a beautifully inspired, fully perfected, symphonic Beethoven masterpiece. What happened? The master stepped in.

Sometimes in life you may not feel like you have the talent, the strength, or the ability, but the good news is God does. When you simply use what you have, no matter how meager or humble it might seem, the Master will show up. God will put His

For we are his workmanship, created in Christ Jesus for good works, which God prepared beforehand, that we should walk in them.

EPHESIANS 2:10 (ESV)

For we are his
workmanship,
created in Christ
Jesus for good
works, which
God prepared
beforehand, that we
should walk in them.

EPHESIANS 2:10 (ESV)

hands over your hands. He will take what you think is average talent, average skills, or average education and transform it into something extraordinary. When the Master steps in, He mixes His excellence with your average and amazing things will begin to happen.

Disovered Treasure

When I began ministering after my father's passing, my sermons were basic, like the little boy playing "Chopsticks." Negative thoughts told me I wasn't a minister, but I countered those doubts with Scripture-based affirmations: "I can do all things through Christ. I'm equipped, anointed, empowered." Instead of talking myself *out* of it, I talked myself *into* it. What happened? The Master stepped in, and God brought out abilities I didn't know I had. The hidden treasure within me began to emerge.

You might believe you don't have what it takes — resources, education, or talent — to fulfill what God has put in your heart. You almost certainly don't, but God does! When you make a move, God makes a move. I faced doubts, nerves, and feelings of inadequacy, but when I stepped out of my safe zone and over into the faith zone, the Master intervened, bringing things out of me I didn't know I had.

He's Got This

In the days ahead, stretching your faith will reveal newfound confidence and abilities within you. Instead of just playing "Chopsticks," you're going to hear the woodwinds join in, bringing supernatural breakthroughs. Just when you think it can't get any better, the brass and the percussion will join in — the right people, the right opportunities. Before long it's going to sound like a beautiful symphony. Recognize it as the Master stepping in, transforming your ordinary into the extraordinary.

Think about this: if your time on earth were up this week, would you have missed out on something amazing? Is your treasure concealed under doubt, fear, or the opinions of others? You owe it to yourself and the world to tap into that hidden treasure. It's never too late, and you're never too old.

Wake up each morning with the assurance that you possess everything you need. Prepare yourself because your hidden treasure is about to emerge.

You owe it to yourself and the world to tap into that hidden treasure. It's never too late, and you're never too old.

JOEL OSTEEN

The Master will blend His supernatural touch with your natural abilities. I declare and believe that before you depart this earth, you will unlock all your potential, allowing your gifts to flourish, and you will become everything God intended you to be.

Declaration Prayer of the Master at Work

Heavenly Father,

With gratitude, I recognize Your power at work within me. There have been moments when I felt lacking in ability, talent, strength, and resources to fulfill Your calling on my life, but I trust that You possess all I need.

Lay Your mighty hands over mine and transform my average and ordinary into the extraordinary. As You infuse Your supernatural touch into my best efforts, I anticipate incredible things unfolding.

I declare and believe that as I advance in faith toward the dreams You've instilled in me, I will fully become the person You intended me to be, fulfilling the dreams You put in my heart.

In Jesus' name, amen.

SECTION 2:
Clear Vision

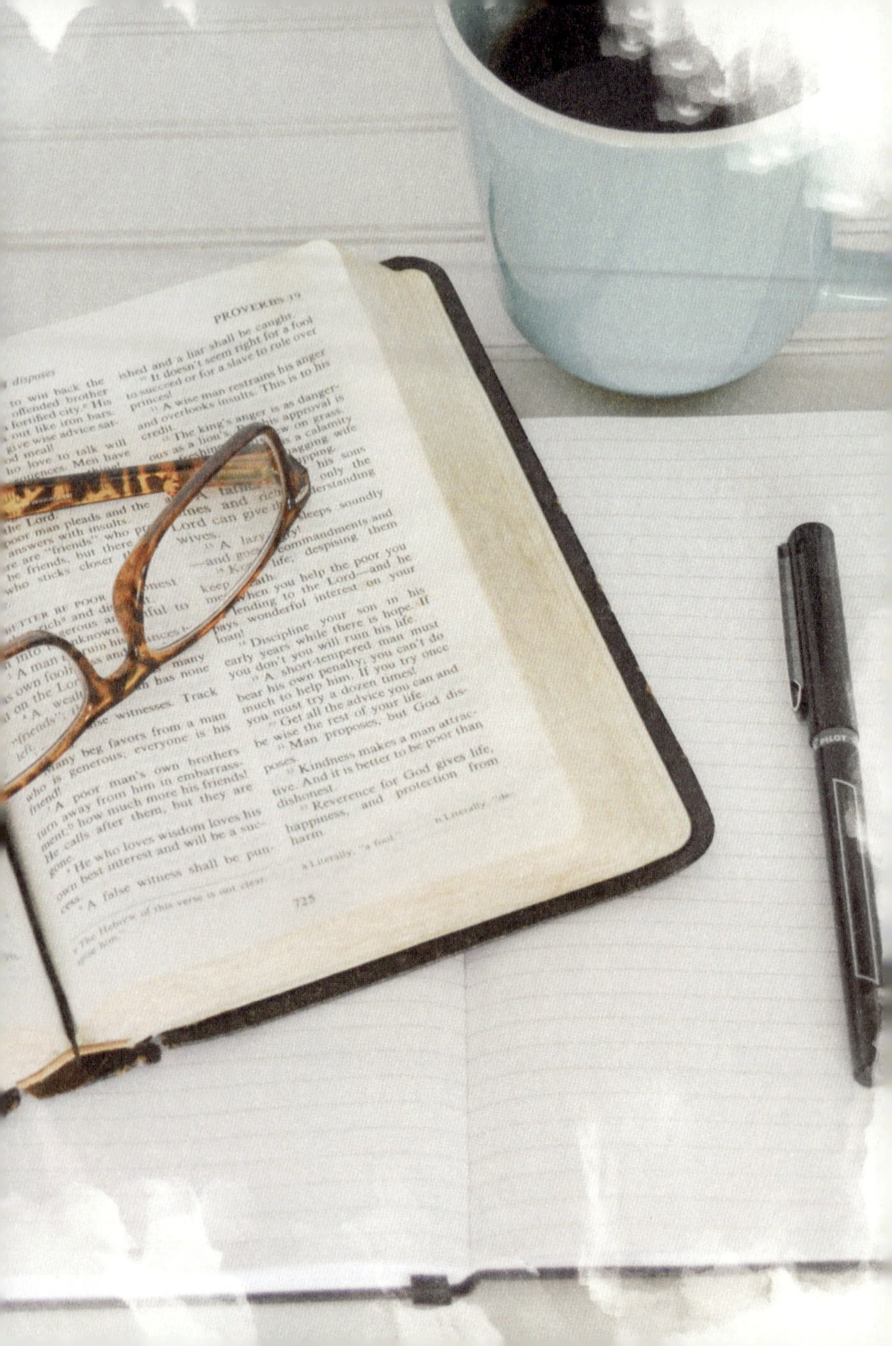
PROVERBS 19
725
PILOT

CHAPTER 7

Images

*Faith shows the reality of what we hope for;
it is the evidence of things we cannot see.*

HEBREWS 11:1 (NLT)

Limited Vision

Many people never reach their potential, not because they're not talented, not because they don't have favor, not because of where they grew up, but simply because their vision is limited. They just don't *see* themselves accomplishing big things, achieving a major goal, or rising to something significant.

It is very unlikely that you'll rise higher than where you see yourself. Through your eyes of faith, you need to see yourself experiencing God's highest and best. That means if you're fighting an illness, you need to see yourself healthy. If you're struggling in your finances, you need to see yourself out of debt, experiencing abundance, and being a blessing to others. If you're dealing with an addiction, see yourself completely and utterly free from those chains. Don't limit the vision of yourself.

A New Image

We need to cultivate a fresh perspective. The images you consistently hold in your mind, within your imagination, shape the direction of your life. Without realizing it, you are drawn toward what you visualize. Highway patrolmen will confirm that when you are driving and stare at something on the road, you tend to hit it. (It's part of what makes their job so hazardous.) You must take your eyes off the object to avoid it. Focus on where you want to go, not where you *don't* want to go. Your vision determines your destination. That's why it's crucial to banish negative images from your thoughts.

You might be wrestling with low self-esteem, feeling inferior and inadequate. It's time to change that mental picture. Align yourself with how God perceives you. He affirms that you are fearfully and wonderfully made, a masterpiece, uniquely crafted. You're adorned with favor, and He has put a robe of approval on you. By changing your mental images, you have the power to change your life. If you think more positively and see yourself as strong, talented, anointed, favored, and with a bright future, you will fulfill your destiny.

Discard the image of a defeated, lonely victim, and instead visualize a restored, blessed, joyful, favored, and emerging-as-better version of yourself. Your life is moving in the direction of how you see yourself.

Make sure the picture you see in your mind is one you really desire.

Envisioning a New Reality

Having a clear vision involves making good choices about the images we allow in our minds. Sometimes while scrolling through my phone, I'll sort through my pictures and start deleting the bad ones. *That one's blurry. That one's not framed right. I don't look good in that one.* Delete, delete, delete.

Have you ever noticed that when you look at a group photo, you tend to zoom in to check how *you* look? If the image doesn't flatter you, even if everyone else looks fantastic, it's a quick decision — delete. We think, *I don't want to see myself that way.*

Now, consider applying the same mindset to the pictures in your mind. When you see an image portraying you as inferior, unattractive, or untalented, adopt the same attitude — delete! *I see myself as valuable, a masterpiece, one of a kind. The image of you being lonely, never meeting anyone, lacking companionship?* Delete. *That's not my future. I envision myself happily married, with children — laughing, loving, and*

When you see an image portraying you as inferior, unattractive, or untalented, adopt the same attitude — delete!

JOEL OSTEEN

dreaming. When a picture emerges of you as sick, weak, or suffering, don't give it any room. Replace it with a new image. See yourself as healthy, strong, vibrant, accomplishing dreams, and enjoying precious moments with your family.

Many desire a better life, yet they can't realize what they don't envision. You must believe it within yourself, and then God can bring it to pass in your external reality.

Creating New Images

When my mother received a diagnosis of terminal cancer, she was very frail. Her skin was yellow, and her voice was weak. From a medical standpoint, there seemed to be no real options for her. You can only imagine the distressing images trying to control her mind. She recounted how, in the dead of night, thoughts whispered, *You can be buried in that new pink dress you bought.* She had to combat these negative images.

To shift her mindset, my mother did something that seemed unusual at the time: she adorned our home with pictures of herself from a time when she was healthy. Wedding photos graced the refrigerator and den. On her bathroom mirror, she had a picture of her with a huge smile, joyfully riding a horse in Montana.

When I returned home from college and noticed all the pictures, I wondered, *Why are all these pictures up?* My mother was crafting a new internal image of herself. When she looked in the mirror, she saw a reflection of potential death, defeat, and illness staring back at her. Instead, when she looked at those images, she saw herself as she wanted to be: healthy, vibrant, enjoying her family, and fulfilling her purpose.

Become What You See

The image you consistently hold in your mind is the direction in which you are moving. Although my mother initially felt weak, she pictured herself as strong. Despite a report of just a few weeks to live, she pictured herself healthy and enjoying a long life. It wasn't an immediate change, but gradually, she began aligning her reality with the positive image she held within. Incredibly, she improved day by day, defying any medical explanation. Today, decades later, she is just like those mental images she saw in her mind—healthy, whole, and vibrant.

Pay attention to the images you entertain. See pictures of yourself blessed, at the forefront and not the tail, lending rather than borrowing. Don't let the dream seem too huge, the giant too big, or the addiction too strong. Picture yourself as capable, a giant killer, a history maker, a barrier breaker.

Declaration Prayer of Images

Heavenly Father,

I come before You with a heart open to change. I declare that I am fearfully and wonderfully made, a masterpiece created with purpose. I cast aside any negative images that do not align with Your vision for my life. Instead, I choose to see myself as strong, anointed, and favored, walking into a bright and fulfilling future.

I surrender any feelings of lack or victim mentality, trusting in Your promise of beauty for ashes and a double return for being treated unfairly. I release the defeated, lonely, and victimized versions of myself and embrace the restored, blessed, joyful, favored, and emerging-as-better individual that You see.

I declare that my inner vision aligns with Your divine image of me. May the pictures in my mind reflect the life I desire, and may Your grace guide me toward the fullness of my destiny.

In Jesus' name, amen.

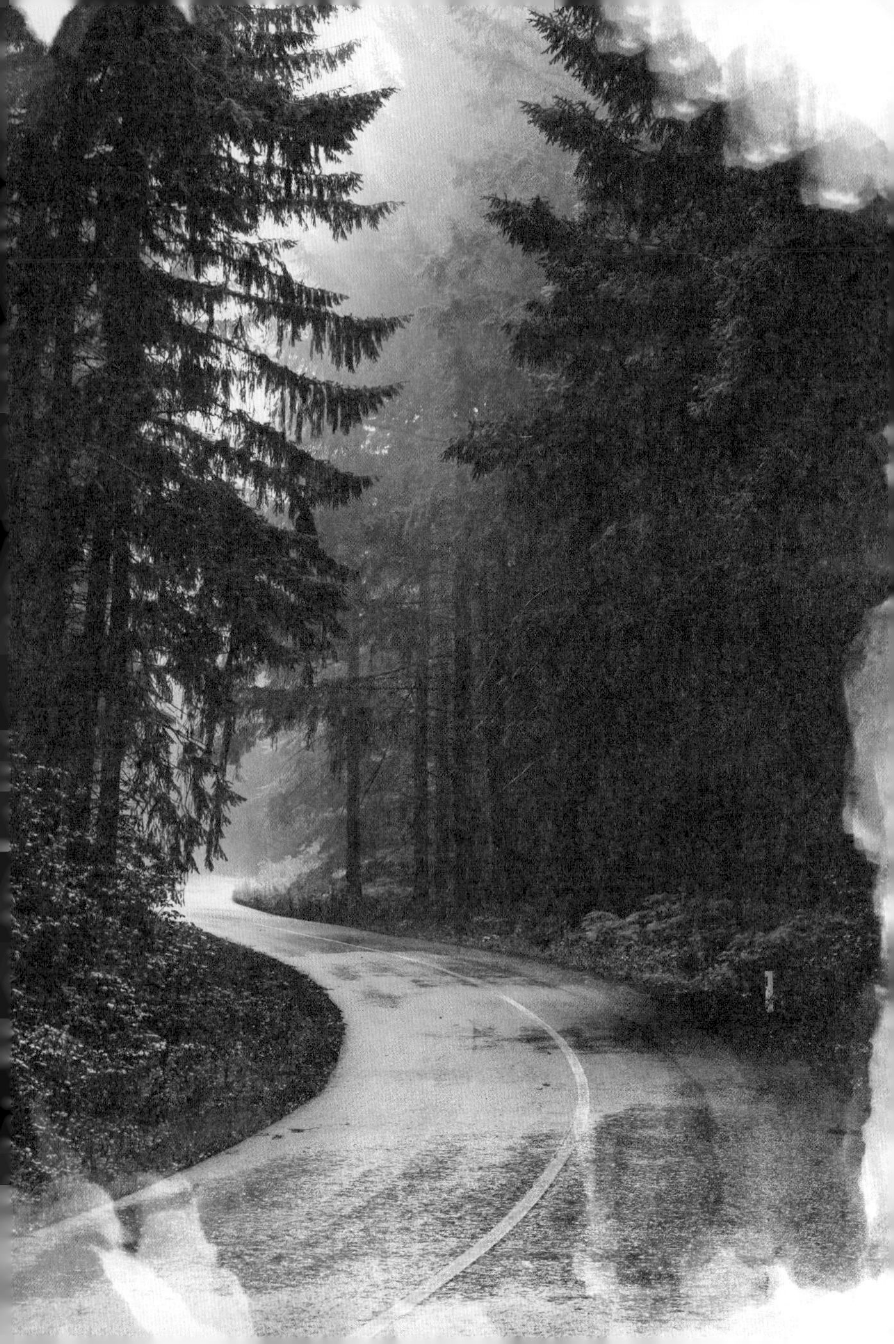

CHAPTER 8
Windshield Wipers

Moreover, the word of the LORD came to me, saying, "Jeremiah, what do you see?" And I said, "I see a branch of an almond tree."

JEREMIAH 1:11 (NKJV)

Blurry Vision

When I was eighteen years old, I found myself driving down the freeway one morning on the way to church. Suddenly, there was a huge downpour. It didn't start gradually or sprinkle lightly; it was as if the heavens had opened. I reached over to turn on my windshield wipers, but to my surprise, nothing happened. I couldn't see a thing. I jiggled the lever, pushed it, and tried everything I could, but still, nothing.

Traveling at sixty miles an hour with zero visibility, I began to panic. Desperate, I rolled down my window, rain hitting my face as I strained to see. Slowly, I began to pull over to the right, driving blindly, praying I wouldn't collide with another car or encounter a ditch or parked vehicle on the shoulder. By the grace of God, the path was clear. I parked and waited for the rain to subside.

My engine was working fine, my tires were in good condition, and my steering was working. I had plenty of gas; the only thing hindering me was my windshield wipers. Despite having all the necessary tools to move forward in my car with all its horsepower, my vision was very blurry. This seemingly minor issue was stopping me from reaching my destination.

Something similar might be true in your life. You're brimming with potential. God has equipped you with gifts, talents, and creativity. He has blessed you with favor and created the right breaks and connections needed to fulfill your purpose. Yet, at times, our vision is hindered by past experiences, negative words, setbacks, and betrayals. The challenge doesn't lie in *who you are.* You are a masterpiece! The challenge lies in *what you can see.*

To see your potential, it's crucial to ensure your "windshield wipers" are in good working order. Constantly clear away hindrances that cloud your vision and prevent you from moving forward.

Wipe it Away

Perhaps you've gotten off course and made some mistakes, and now guilt and shame are attempting to hinder your vision. They whisper, *You don't deserve blessings; look at what you did. You're unworthy; just accept where you are at.* Reject those lies; get your windshield wipers working. You are forgiven.

God's mercy overcomes your mistakes; He doesn't dwell on the negatives of your past. It's your responsibility now to clear out the guilt and shame.

Start seeing yourself as worthy, forgiven, and a cherished child of the Most High God. Maybe discouragement has cast a film over your windshield due to past disappointments and wrongs committed by others. It's easy to let those experiences cloud your vision for your future and lead to a lack of belief in better things and improvement. The Enemy aims to limit your vision so that you remain unaware of the amazing future that lies ahead. Now, get your windshield wipers working. Your best days are yet to come.

What Do You See?

Jeremiah faced a similar challenge. God had a big plan for his life — to speak to nations and shape culture. God selected him to stand against nations and kingdoms, to uproot, tear down, destroy, overthrow, build up, and plant. Yet, Jeremiah, being young and feeling unqualified, initially made excuses: "I can't speak to nations; I'm too young,

Your best days are yet to come.

JOEL OSTEEN

and I wouldn't know what to say." However, God assured him, "Don't worry, I will put My words in your mouth."

God said to him, *"Today I appoint you to stand up against nations and kingdoms. Some you must uproot and tear down, destroy and overthrow. Others you must build up and plant"* (Jeremiah 1:10, NLT). Jeremiah struggled with his calling, unable to see himself in that role. God never requires something without providing the ability to fulfill it.

Despite God's prophecy of an incredible future where he would impact nations, it all came down to a key question, "Jeremiah, what do you see?"

Growth

Doubt, fear, and insecurity distorted his vision until a prophecy shifted his perspective. *Moreover, the word of the LORD came to me, saying, "Jeremiah, what do you see?" And I said, "I see a branch of an almond tree"* (Jeremiah 1:11, NKJV). He saw growth and new opportunities to step into new levels. As his vision cleared, he went on to fulfill God's plan, impacting nations and flourishing as God promised.

Similarly, God has given us remarkable promises: protection, restoration, prosperity, and more. Yet, God is asking, "What do you see?" Your perception of yourself, your future, and your circumstances will determine the outcome. Turn on your wipers. Clear out doubts and excuses and see yourself the way God sees you — well-able, strong, favored, and victorious.

In my own journey, stepping up to pastor Lakewood Church after my father's passing seemed beyond my capabilities. I lacked training and experience, preferring to stay behind the scenes. However, accepting the new things God had in store was crucial. His dream for our lives is much larger than our own.

Like Jeremiah, I had to quit seeing myself as limited and unqualified. Despite voices of doubt and clouded futures, I kept my spiritual "windshield wipers" going, declaring, "I can do all things through Christ. I'm equipped, empowered, anointed." Through eyes of faith, I saw excellence, church growth, and people being helped—conceiving the new image God planted in my heart. Breakthroughs are coming, favor is coming, and so is healing, restoration, and the fullness of your destiny.

Declaration Prayer of Clear Vision

Heavenly Father,

I come to You with a heart filled with gratitude and reverence. I declare that I desire for my vision to agree with Your divine purpose for my life. I cast aside any doubt, fear, or insecurity that distorts the image You have of me. I affirm that, through Christ, I am well-able, strong, and victorious. I desire to clear away all hindrances so I can see myself as You see me — equipped, empowered, and anointed for the incredible journey You have planned.

Lord, I seek Your guidance to see the future You have prepared for me. Grant me the clarity of vision to recognize the growth and new opportunities sprouting in my life. I declare that, through my eyes of faith, I see myself excelling, overcoming challenges, and walking in the abundant life You promised.

Father, I acknowledge the vastness of Your promises in my life — protection, restoration, prosperity, and a future filled with hope. I declare that these promises are not just words but a reality that I embrace through faith. May my life be a testimony to Your faithfulness and grace.

In Jesus' name, amen.

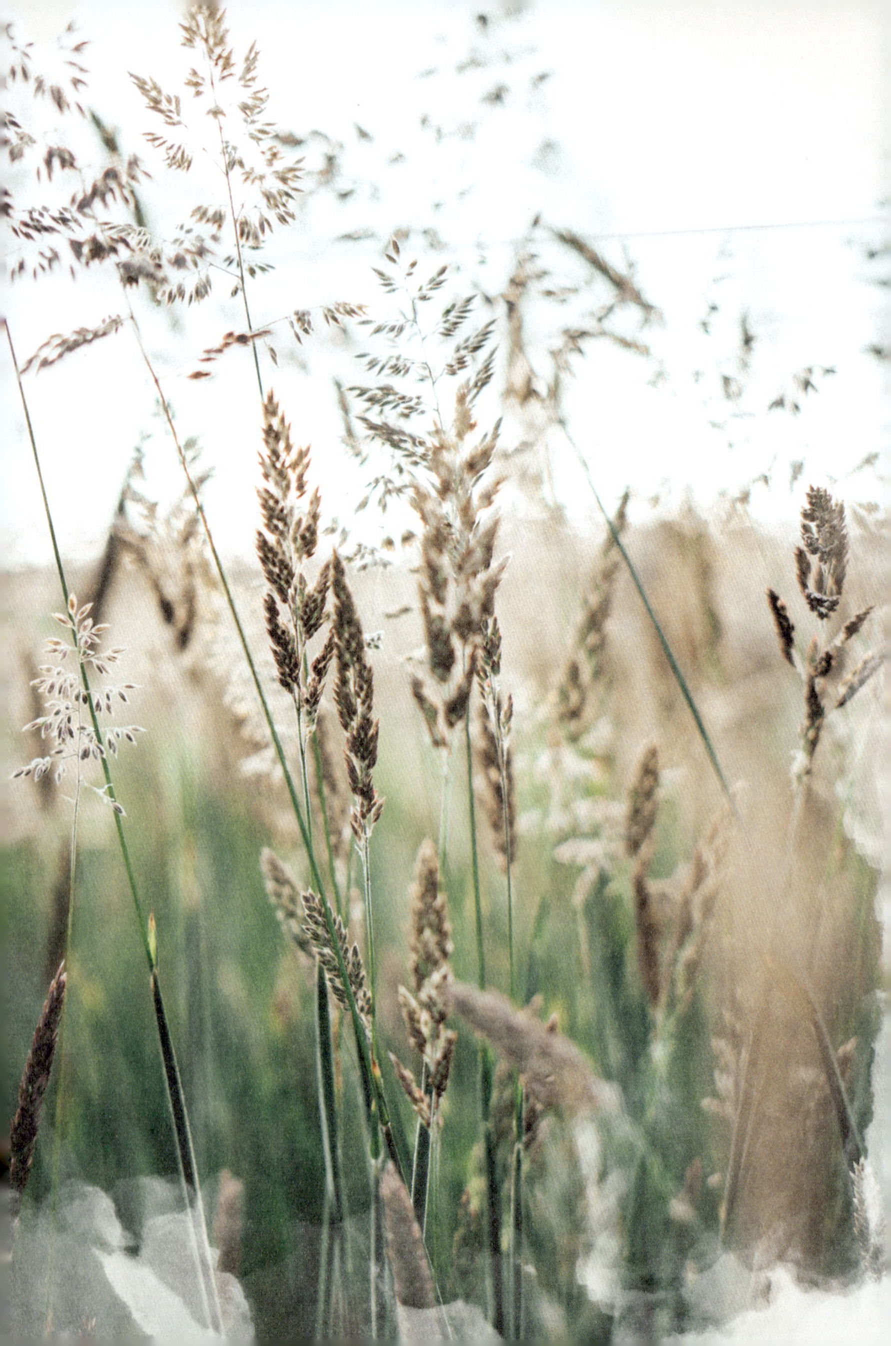

CHAPTER 9
Grasshoppers

So they spread this bad report about the land among the Israelites: "The land we traveled through and explored will devour anyone who goes to live there. All the people we saw were huge. We even saw giants there, the descendants of Anak. Next to them we felt like grasshoppers, and that's what they thought, too!"

NUMBERS 13:32-33 (NLT)

Distorted Perspective

To have clear vision of your dreams and purpose it's so important to remember that others don't control your destiny — only God does. Don't let negative comments blur your vision for something better.

Remember when Moses sent twelve men to spy out the Promised Land, ten of them returned with a negative report. They said, *"We even saw giants there, the descendants of Anak. Next to them we felt like grasshoppers, and that's what they thought, too!"* (Numbers 13:33, NLT). Their perspective was distorted. They viewed the opposition as giants, powerful and undefeatable. They saw themselves as weak, lacking in size, talent, and experience. However, in reality, they possessed the favor of God and were destined to conquer the land. The problem lay in their blurred windshield and distorted view.

Grasshoppers

It's interesting that they viewed themselves as grasshoppers. A grasshopper has wings, but its flight is limited — it can't cover long distances. The Enemy wants you to see yourself the same way, with restricted potential and as a fragile little thing that can't go very high or very far. There will always be voices that suggest you're just a grasshopper, incapable of achieving greatness due to circumstances and obstacles.

Here's the truth. Isaiah 40:31 tells us that those who hope in the Lord will soar on wings like eagles! You were created to soar, rise above challenges, and overcome obstacles. So, the key question is whether you see yourself as a grasshopper or as an eagle.

If you think, *People at work dislike me, and I'll never get that promotion,* you're aligning with a grasshopper mindset that keeps you grounded. The Israelites wandered in the desert for forty years because they saw themselves as limited and lacking and didn't take their promise as God intended. Don't let this grasshopper image hinder your ability to soar.

Soar Don't Hop

I'll never get ahead, especially with the cost of living and inflation. How could I ever pay off my house? What you're expressing is a grasshopper mentality. The Enemy wants you to believe you're limited, at a disadvantage — unable to fly, be happy, get married, or achieve your goals. What if, instead, you discovered that the wings by your side aren't those of a grasshopper but of an eagle?

Consider this: What's holding you back may not be external circumstances, other people, or your upbringing, but rather how you perceive yourself. Imagine if your windshield wipers started working, your vision cleared, and you began to see yourself as you truly are — a child of the Most High God. You were created to reign in life, to be healthy, strong, confident, valuable, and to achieve dreams while overcoming obstacles.

I urge you to discard that grasshopper image and embrace the way God sees you. Despite disappointments, bad breaks, and mistakes, get your windshield wipers working. Today is a new day. Clear out the doubt, disregard what people have said, and eliminate bitterness and thinking you're average. Nothing that has happened to you has derailed God's purpose for your life. As your vision clears, you'll step into new levels of favor and blessing meant for you.

... those who hope in the LORD will renew their strength. They will soar on wings like eagles; they will run and not grow weary, they will walk and not be faint.

ISAIAH 40:31 (NIV)

... those who hope in the LORD will renew their strength. They will soar on wings like eagles; they will run and not grow weary, they will walk and not be faint.

ISAIAH 40:31 (NIV)

You were created to reign in life,
to be healthy, strong, confident,
valuable, and to achieve dreams while
overcoming obstacles.

JOEL OSTEEN

Which Dream Do You Believe?

About three months after my father's passing, when I was nervous and struggling for courage to keep going, I had a dream or, rather, a nightmare. In this dream, the church was full but as I stepped up to speak, everyone silently got up and walked out of the building. Right on cue, without saying a word, the congregation just filed out the doors. It was such a vivid dream that I woke up in a cold sweat.

Let me tell you: the Enemy works tirelessly to put negative, defeating images inside us. The Scripture emphasizes casting down wrong imaginations, discarding those harmful mental pictures. Pay attention to what drains your faith, makes you insecure, or intimidates you. These are imaginations you need to delete to prevent them from distorting your vision.

A few months before my father's passing, my wife, Victoria, had a friend who shared with her a dream she had. In it, she saw me speaking in front of a vast stadium filled with people, all weeping. In her dream, I was comforting and leading them, and everyone was listening intently. A dream completely opposite of the nightmare I had.

Between these two dreams — I chose to believe the positive one because it was in line with what I knew God had for me. I allowed that positive image to take root and sprout within me.

You have the power to choose which images influence you. You can see yourself as defeated, stuck, failing, or not enough. You can also see yourself prospering, rising higher, accomplishing new goals, and setting new standards. At times, like in my experience, you'll need to enlarge your vision. God didn't create you to reach one level and get stuck. Be open to greater things, see yourself at new levels, going where you've never gone and doing what you've never imagined possible.

People may tell you that your dreams are unattainable. Tune out those voices that can undermine your faith and confidence. They can't see what you see. God planted the dream in you, not in them. Now, do your part and see the increase, abundance, and possibilities that lie ahead.

Declaration Prayer of Clear Vision

Heavenly Father,

I come before You with a heart filled with gratitude and determination. Today, I declare that I will not be held back by negative images or defeating thoughts. I cast down every wrong image that seeks to distort my vision and drain my faith. I choose to delete the imaginations that make me shrink back, feel insecure, or feel intimidated. Instead, I embrace the positive images that align with Your promises for my life.

Lord, I choose to believe in the dreams and visions You have for me. I reject the grasshopper mentality and embrace the truth that I am an eagle created to soar above challenges. I declare that doubt and insecurity have no place in my life, and I open myself to the greater things You have in store for me.

Lord, grant me the wisdom to keep my spiritual windshield wipers going, clearing away doubts and distortions. Help me see the increase, abundance, and possibilities that You have planted within me. I trust in Your promises, and I believe that as my vision clears, I will step into new levels of favor and blessing.

In Jesus' name, amen.

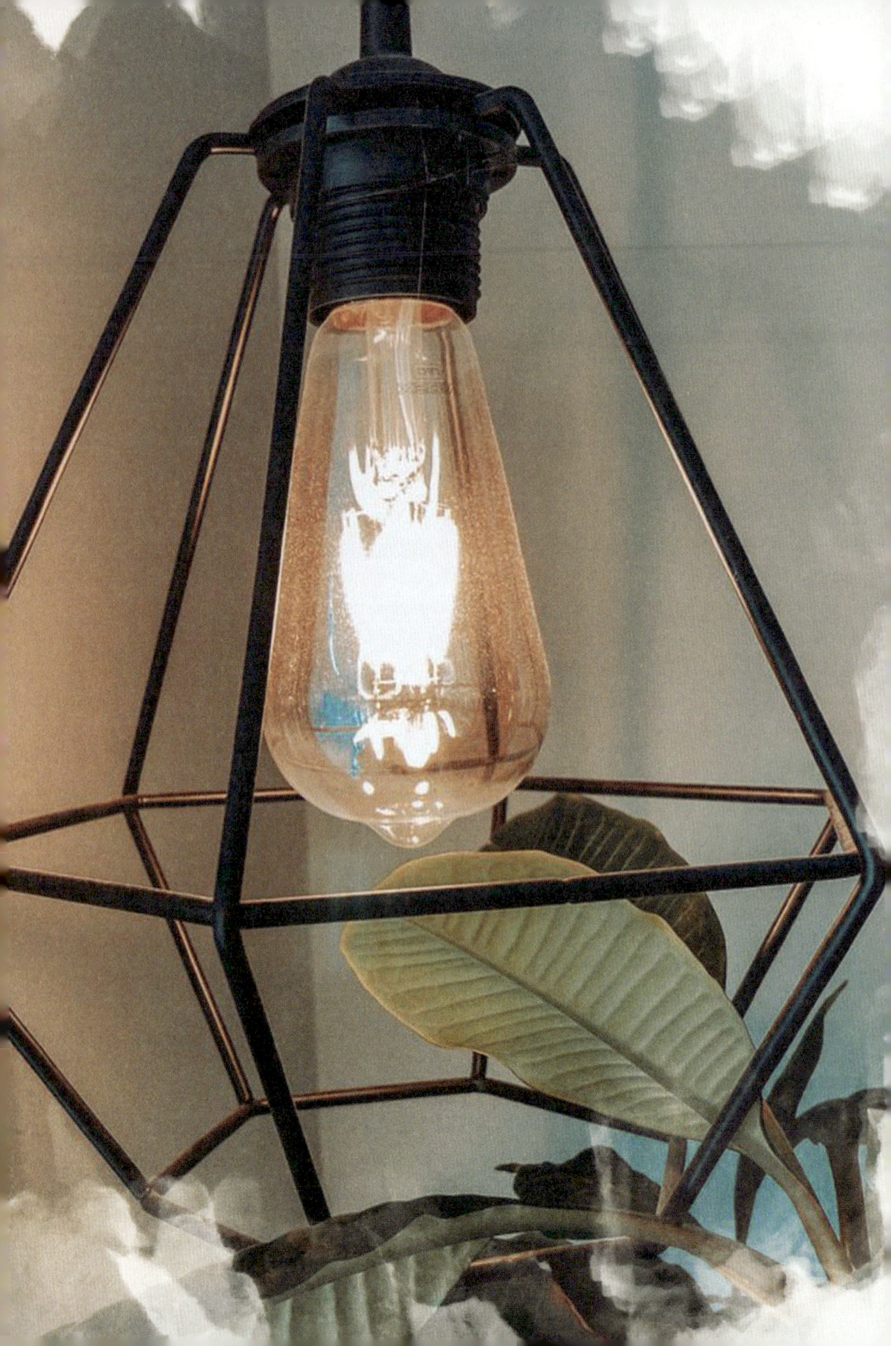

CHAPTER 10

Imagine

The eyes of your understanding being enlightened; that ye may know what is the hope of his calling, and what the riches of the glory of his inheritance in the saints.

EPHESIANS 1:18 (KJV)

Inner Eyesight

How is your inner eyesight? Has your vision been clouded by the words of others? I once heard a story from a woman who attended a job interview for a position she deeply desired. Despite being qualified and well-trained, she was told, "I'm sorry, you just don't have the personality for this job. You're not outgoing enough." Instead of recognizing her worth, she allowed those words to cast a shadow over her vision and believed she was lacking and not up to par.

I shared with her what I'm sharing with you now. Negative statements like "You're too small," "You're too young," "You're not talented enough," and "You don't have what it takes" do not determine your calling. God does.

In this chapter's key scripture, the apostle Paul prays that the eyes of our understanding would be enlightened. Why? So we can see the amazing future God has for us. A hopeful future! The Amplified Bible says it this way: *And [I pray] that the eyes of your heart [the very center and core of your being] may be enlightened [flooded with light by the Holy Spirit], so that you will know and cherish the hope [the divine guarantee, the confident expectation] to which He has called you* (Ephesians 1:18, AMP).

Paul prayed for you to have profound knowledge and understanding to brighten the very center of your being, allowing you to see what God sees. He prayed for clear vision with the "eyes" of our understanding so that we may see and embrace the hope and divine calling that God has given us.

I Can Only Imagine

When a friend of mine was vacationing in Hawaii, their guide took them around to explore the sights. At one point, they reached a location where the guide pointed to the top of a hill that showcased a stunning house with a panoramic view of the ocean, surrounded by palm trees, lush green grass, and expansive windows. It resembled a postcard — truly beautiful. In passing, my friend remarked to the guide, "I can't even imagine living in a house like that."

To his surprise, he heard a voice saying, *Don't worry, you never will.* Startled, he wondered if it was God speaking. He sensed God saying, "Yes, son, it's Me.

As long as you can't imagine it, as long as you can't see it, it's never going to happen."

This encounter made him reflect on how many of us might be missing out on the great things God has in store because we can't imagine them. *I can't imagine having a successful year in my business with inflation, the stock market down. I can't imagine my health turning around with what the doctors told me. I can't imagine my children doing anything great.* Instead of letting your imagination work against you, consider looking through the eyes of faith and allowing your imagination to work for you.

See What Is Not Yet

Recently, I heard an inspiring news story about a woman whose family home in Maui was burned to the ground by a raging wildfire. Her heart sank to learn that all their possessions — clothes, furniture, computers, and cherished keepsakes — were reduced to ashes. Yet, with this terrible news, her faith saw a different picture: a new, improved home, and her family singing, sharing meals as Hawaiian families have for generations. She held to her faith in God and refused to give in to despair or fear.

Christians can triumph over sad situations because they see reality through a different lens. They do not dwell on the past or rely solely on the tangible. You are one of these individuals, guided by faith in Jesus. Your trust rests in Him. He is your source of strength, and He holds your future. This enables you to move forward in faith and not by what you see.

Faith gives you the ability to see the "not yet" and the "what will be." It sees the dream and has the confidence that it will come to pass. Hebrews 11:1 (AMP) puts it this way: *Now faith is the assurance (title deed, confirmation) of things hoped for (divinely guaranteed), and the evidence of things not seen [the conviction of their reality—faith comprehends as fact what cannot be experienced by the physical senses].*

Faith Glasses

Faith is a strong belief in God's power and His promise of a brighter future. When God makes a promise, He guarantees it and your faith confirms it. It is complete trust and total dependence on what

God has said and what He will do. Faith convinces us that things we can't see really exist.

Put on faith glasses. Through these spiritual lenses, you can clearly see God's hand in every aspect of your life. Expect answered prayers and the miracles that are on the way. With faith, you can see your Heavenly Father's active presence, working out breakthroughs for His children.

Imagine That

We should adopt a mindset free from our human limits. The right attitude is to boldly say, "It may seem unlikely, but I can imagine myself getting healthy. Like God did for Joel's mom, I can imagine defying the odds, running, playing, and living a long life." "I can picture paying off my house, expanding my business, and leaving an inheritance for my children's children."

For those who are single and desiring marriage, even after a long wait, resist the Enemy's attempt to paint a picture of loneliness and discouragement. Instead say, "I can imagine myself happily married. I can see someone incredible — Godly, attractive, fun, friendly, and financially prosperous. I can picture a life filled with laughter, love, and a blessed marriage."

"I can imagine my children excelling. I can see them leaving their mark and doing great things." "Yes, I've had this addiction for a long time, but I can picture myself breaking free. I can see myself being whole and clean."

God is going to take you further than you've ever imagined, but it has to start on the inside. What do you see? What image do you have of yourself, your family, your finances, your future? You're moving toward the picture you have in your mind.

Maybe you're limited right now because you're not seeing the right things. Your vision has been clouded. My encouragement is to get new glasses. Clear out all the negative, limited, not-enough, too-big, never-going-to-happen thoughts, and go back to what God says about you in His Word.

See yourself as blessed, prosperous, healthy, in shape, achieving goals, building the Kingdom, and being a blessing. Don't imagine yourself as a grasshopper with wings but can't fly far. Imagine yourself as an eagle — soaring, overcoming, accomplishing, a victor and never a victim.

God is about to step in and do something unusual. New doors are about to open, negative situations are turning around.

Declaration Prayer of Faith

Heavenly Father,

I desire to have a greater ability to imagine the possibilities of what You can do. I can see my children excelling, leaving their mark, and doing great things. I see myself breaking free from long-standing addictions, becoming whole and clean. Despite negative economic reports, I choose faith, picturing a year filled with blessings, productivity, abundance, and favor.

I clear my vision of limits and negative thoughts, trusting in Your promises. I see myself blessed, prosperous, healthy, achieving goals, building Your Kingdom, and being a blessing.

God, I ask You to step in and do the unusual. Open new doors; turn negative situations around. Bring breakthroughs, favor, healing, restoration, and the fulfillment of my God-given dreams.

In Jesus' name, amen.

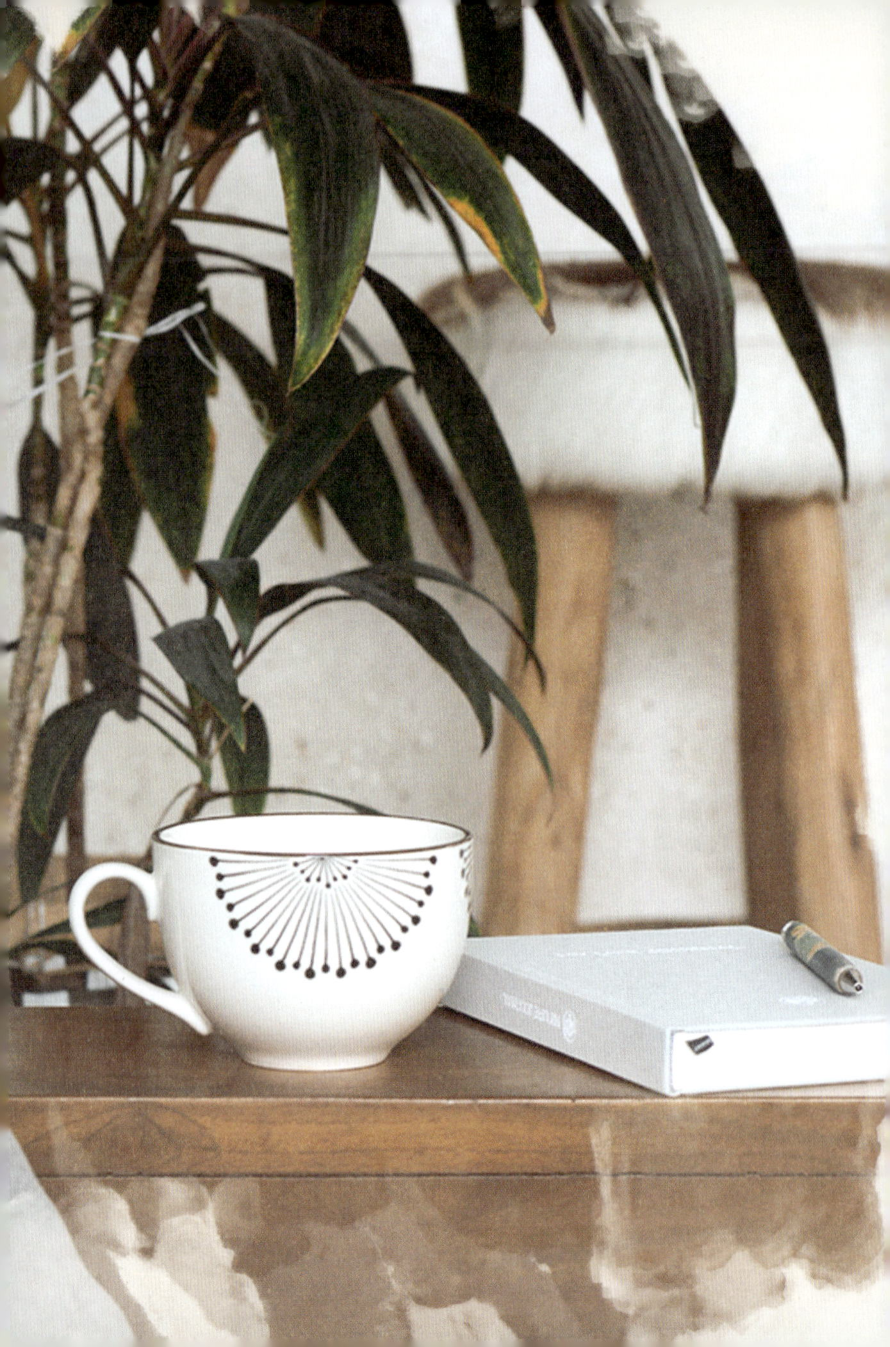

CHAPTER 11
A Promise

*For God had promised,
"I will return about this time next year,
and Sarah will have a son."*

ROMANS 9:9 (NLT)

Dreams Are a Promise

When God gives you a dream, when He puts a promise in your heart, that doesn't mean it's going to come to pass without opposition, delays, and adversities. There will be things you don't understand. You'll have plenty of opportunities to get discouraged or frustrated and think it's never going to happen. *I must have heard God wrong. Nothing is going right.* In those tough times, you must do like Joseph and remember your dream.

It's vital to remember: God didn't bring you this far to leave you! You may not understand it, but God is in control. He's directing your steps. Now do your part, keep your faith, keep a good attitude. Let God be your vindicator. Let God fight your battles. He has it all figured out. "Well, Joel, I'm in the pits. I don't understand it." "A friend lied about me." "I went through a divorce." "I lost a loved one." Don't get bitter; it's just a detour on the way to your destiny. The promise is still on track.

Not Genetics

It's important to remember that your promise is not about anything in the natural. It wasn't passed on by your parents or grandparents. The promise God has given you is of the Spirit and comes directly from Him. It has nothing to do with your upbringing, your genes, or your ancestors. Your identity and destiny are totally determined by God.

Paul said in Romans 9:9 (NLT) about the promise God gave Abraham: *For God had promised, "I will return about this time next year, and Sarah will have a son."* He was saying that it wasn't Abraham's sperm that gave identity here but God's promise. His promise was more powerful than biology and genetics! The Israelite nation's identity was not determined by race but by what God promised to Sarah. It was a promise that took priority over genetics.

Your genes don't determine your promise — God does. He gave it and you can be sure He will fulfill it. We need to make good and right decisions, but God is not going to point a finger at you if the promise is not fulfilled. The promise depends on Him. It rests on His shoulders.

It is comforting to know that while our futures may sometimes seem unclear, and sometimes our dreams feel distant and futile, God knows precisely what lies ahead. He not only designed us, but He also designed and created every day of our lives before we were born.

Some of those days may be influenced by the curse on the earth, Satanic strategies, our free will, and desires of the flesh putting us off course from God's original design. The bad things that come to us in life are the result of fallen humanity living on a broken planet, but through it all, God's hand is still just as steady, and He will faithfully lead us.

Dormant

The scripture says in 2 Corinthians 4:17 (NKJV), *For our light affliction, which is but for a moment.* When you face opposition and things don't go your way, recognize that it's not permanent. That's not your final destination. Quit worrying about things that are only temporary. Like Joseph, the pit is temporary, the betrayal is temporary; the injustice, the

. . . through it all, God's hand is still just as steady, and He will faithfully lead us.

JOEL OSTEEN

loneliness — that's not your permanent home. It's a temporary stop.

Psalm 84:6 (AMP) says, *Passing through the Valley of Weeping*. It doesn't say settling in the Valley of Weeping, getting stuck in the valley, or building your house in the valley. The valley is temporary; you're passing through it. Now, my challenge to you is to quit losing sleep over a temporary stop. Quit being stressed out over something that's only for a season; it's not permanent.

I was in my backyard one time, and my grass looked dead. It was brown and patchy. I called the man who helps me with my landscape and said, "What happened to my grass? Why did it die?" He said, "Joel, it's not dead; it's just not in season. It's fully alive but dormant right now. In a few months, it will be as green and full as can be."

I was worried over something that was temporary. I thought that was the way it was always going to be. Once I realized that was normal, I never worried about it again. When I saw that brown grass, I thought, *It's just a matter of time before it's back to green.*

Temporary

Are you worrying about things that are only temporary, letting something steal your joy because you think it's over and it's never going to work out? Let me tell you: your dream is not dead, it's just not in season. Your time is coming. The right people, the right opportunities, healing, and restoration are headed your way. Remember, 2 Corinthians 4:17 says these light afflictions are temporary. The verse goes on to say... *is working for us a far more exceeding and eternal weight of glory* (NKJV). The affliction is temporary, but the glory is much longer lasting.

Friend, stir up what's on the inside. You may have a promised dream that is dormant; it is only temporary. Start thanking God that it's coming to pass. Maybe you're on a detour right now, something you don't understand. Don't get discouraged; you're just passing through.

It's easy to remember the hurt and disappointment. I'm asking you to remember the dream and the promise. If you will do this, I believe and declare that dreams that are dormant are coming back to life. Promises you've given up on are being resurrected.

Like He did for Joseph, God is going to turn every stumbling block into a stepping-stone. You will rise higher, accomplish your goals, and become everything you were created to be, in Jesus' name.

Declaration Prayer of Promise

Heavenly Father,

Thank You for reminding me that the challenges I face are temporary, merely short stops on my journey. Like Joseph, I declare that the pits, betrayals, injustices, and loneliness are passing phases, and I rebuke any fear or worry associated with them.

As Psalm 84:6 says, I affirm that I am merely passing through Valley of Weeping — not settling or building my home there. Grant me the strength to not lose sleep or be stressed over temporary seasons. I declare that dreams and promises You've given me that seem dormant will come back to life. I trust in Your perfect timing and believe that what may appear lifeless now is simply awaiting its appointed season of renewal. In Jesus' name, I declare victory in my temporary challenges and look forward to the fulfillment of Your promises.

In Jesus' name, amen.

SECTION 3:
Promises

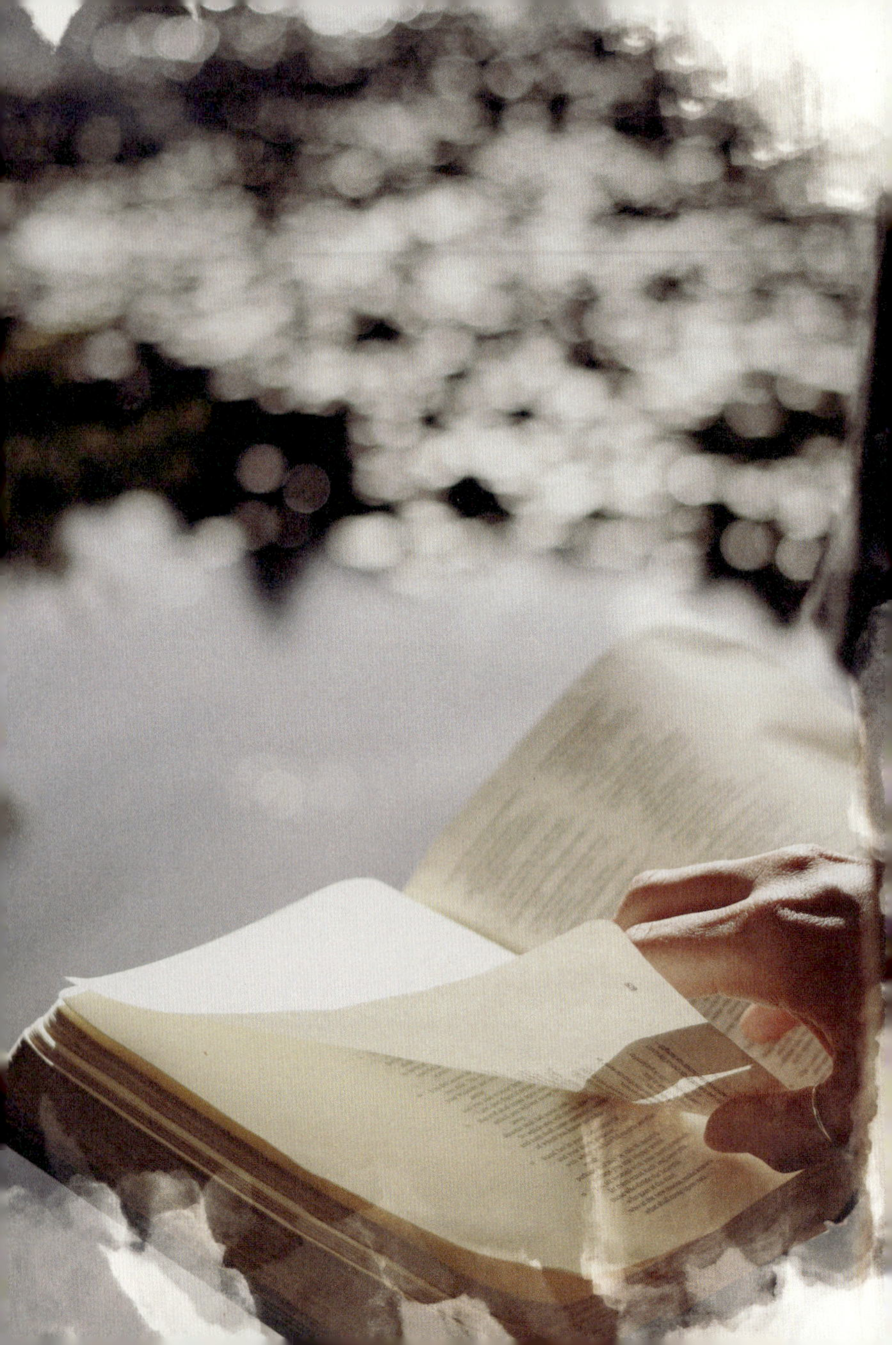

CHAPTER 12

What He Said

*Let us firmly hold the profession
of our faith without wavering,
for He who promised is faithful.*

HEBREWS 10:23 (MEV)

A Mental Battle

We all hold promises in our hearts, dreams from God we are meant to fulfill. Yet, there will still likely be challenges to overcome. There may be a time when you are confident that it will all unfold. You've prayed fervently, believed wholeheartedly, and carried a passionate conviction. Then, in spite of all that, the journey takes longer than expected. Then disappointments arise and support fails. Maybe the medical reports don't improve and negative thoughts grow. In those moments, it's crucial to hold onto the initial thing God told you. That's when you must maintain faith in the original promise.

Before Jesus raised Lazarus from the dead, He said to Martha, *"Did I not tell you that if you believed you would see the glory of God?"* (John 11:40, ESV). You may be facing sickness, feeling worried and stressed out. God is saying, "Did I not tell you that I will restore health to you? Did I not tell you that by My stripes you are healed? Did I not tell you that the number of your days I will fulfill?" Start thanking God for what He told you instead of letting negative thoughts plague your mind.

Start thanking God for what He told you instead of letting negative thoughts plague your mind.

JOEL OSTEEN

There's a battle taking place in our minds. The Enemy comes against us with thoughts of doubt, fear, and worry. His goal is to keep your mind filled with all the negative so you're too preoccupied with what's not going to work out.

Take control of your thought life. When worry comes, don't let it dominate your mind. Stay on the offensive. Purposely remember what God said. Thank Him that He's making a way. Thank Him that He always causes you to triumph. Thank Him that what was meant for your harm, He's turning for your good. Thank Him that He's taking you from glory to glory, from victory to victory.

Check the Instruments

A friend of mine knew an older gentleman who was a fighter pilot in World War II. He not only flew missions but was also a flight trainer. Before taking young pilots up, he stressed the importance of always flying the plane by the instruments, not by what they saw. They spent months on the ground in flight simulators, flying planes strictly by the instruments.

"Did I not tell you that if you believed you would see the glory of God?"

JOHN 11:40 (ESV)

"Did I not tell you that if you believed you would see the glory of God?"

JOHN 11:40 (ESV)

After a young pilot completed the program, the instructor took him up in the air. The pilot performed well, with everything running smoothly, just as in his training. However, a few minutes later, a storm suddenly arose, and they found themselves in bad weather — dark clouds and the plane bouncing around. It reached a point where they couldn't see anything.

The young pilot panicked, feeling the plane shaking. He became disoriented and confused, unable to determine whether he was gaining or losing altitude. Straining to see out the window for a visual sign of the right direction, he neglected his instruments. Then the flight instructor took a blanket used to cover the windshield during storage and clipped it in place. Now, the young pilot couldn't see anything and had no choice but to rely on the instruments. In a few minutes, they emerged from the storm and eventually landed the plane safely.

Sometimes, like this young pilot, we know what God promised us; we have the instruments, but we look out the window. You can't go by what you see, or you'll get discouraged. Go back to your instruments. Remember what God promised you.

We do well on the ground; it's easy to believe then. But when the storm hits in flight, we start looking at the clouds and winds. It's bumpy; we don't see a way out. When we're under pressure and life gets stressful, it's easy to focus on the wrong things. Too often, we panic and worry, but we must come back to the instruments. Are you focused on the storm, or are you focused on what God promised you?

He's spoken dreams to your heart. He's whispered things to you in the night. The Enemy has tried to drown them out with stormy circumstances, but they are still alive. What God started He's going to finish. Now do your part and remember what He said. Keep declaring what He promised, keep thanking Him for it.

What Did He Say?

When you're under pressure, it's so important to filter what you're allowing to play in your mind. You must go back to what God said — not what people said, not what the experts said, not what your mind says, not how you feel. Maybe you're discouraged over how long it's taking for your dream to come to fruition, how it looks impossible.

Keep declaring what He promised,
keep thanking Him for it.

JOEL OSTEEN

God is saying, "Did I not tell you what I started I will finish?" "Did I not tell you, if you delight yourself in Me, I will give you the desires of your heart?" The medical report wasn't good, now you're upset. "Did I not tell you no weapon formed against you will prosper?" People at the office are playing politics, trying to push you down; they have more influence, more seniority.

"Did I not tell you when the Enemy comes in like a flood, I will raise up a barrier?" "Did I not tell you I will fight your battles for you?" "Did I not tell you I am preparing a table before you in the presence of your enemies?" When you remember what God said, you won't be worried. You'll have peace during the storm. You'll have faith to believe for the impossible. You'll have the courage to defeat giants, the endurance to outlast opposition, the favor to accomplish more than you thought possible. We must navigate toward our destinies by what He said.

For He who promised is faithful.

Declaration Prayer of God's Promise

Heavenly Father,

I am so grateful for the promises and dreams You've placed within me. In the face of challenges, disappointments, and unexpected delays, I declare that Your promises remain steadfast and unwavering. In moments of sickness, worry, and stress, I choose to remember and declare Your healing promises, trusting that by Your stripes we are healed, and the number of our days You will fulfill.

Lord, during life's storms, I recognize the battle for my thoughts. I declare victory over doubt, fear, and worry. Like a skilled pilot relying on instruments during turbulence, I commit to trusting Your promises as my guiding instruments. I will not be swayed by what I see or feel but will focus on Your Word.

I declare that what You started in my life You will bring to completion. With a heart full of faith and gratitude, I thank You for turning difficulties into opportunities, leading me from glory to glory and victory to victory.

In Jesus' name, amen.

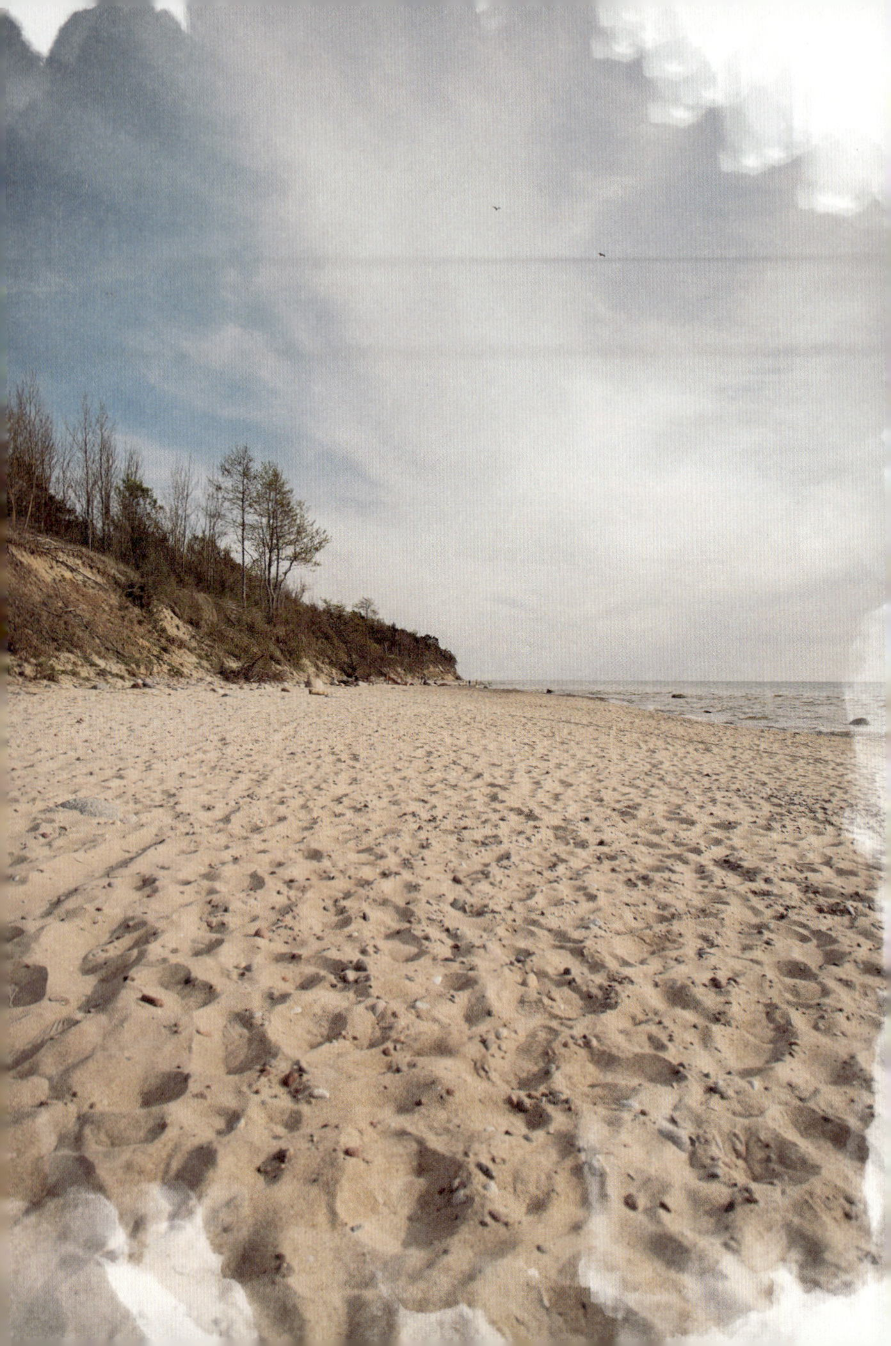

CHAPTER 13
Sing to It

*Then Israel sang this song: "Spring up,
O well! All of you sing to it."*

NUMBERS 21:17 (NKJV)

Promise in our Hearts

All of us have things we're believing for. Dreams we want to accomplish. Problems we're hoping will turn around. We know God put the promise in our hearts, but we don't see how it can happen. The obstacles seem too great. The opponents seem too strong. Our resources seem too meager. Our circumstances seem too hard.

Dry Well

This is the way the Israelites felt in Numbers 21. They were out in the desert in the middle of a drought. They were hot, tired, and thirsty. All they could see was more sand, rocks, barrenness. Just when they thought they were done, they came to a place where there was an old well. I can imagine they were so excited, thinking, *We're finally going to have some water.* They rushed over to it and looked in, but the well was dry.

They could see it hadn't been used in years. It was filled in with dirt and sand, all kinds of debris, yet another disappointment. But God told Moses to gather the people around, and He would give them water.

He gave them the promise that water was coming in the desert, and things were about to turn around! But the promise didn't automatically come to pass. It didn't happen just because God said it. There was something the Israelites had to do.

Sing to It

The key scripture from Numbers 21:17 (NKJV) says, *Then Israel sang this song: "Spring up, O well."* Right in the middle of the desert, with circumstances that looked impossible, feeling discouraged and thirsty. Filled with disappointment, instead of complaining, they obeyed and began to sing, "Spring up, O well."

The Israelites were making a declaration of faith. They were saying, "Lord, thank You that water is coming, thank You that You're making streams in the desert, thank You that You're supplying our needs." Then the end of verse 17 says, *Sing to it.* That was the key to receiving the promise of water.

This is an example for us. You must sing to your promise. It didn't make sense in the natural for the Israelites; the well was empty, every circumstance said water was not going to come out of a dried-up well. Their thoughts told them, *You're wasting your time, you look foolish singing to a well.* They could have talked themselves out of it and said, "Moses, we're hot and thirsty. We'll sing after we see the water; we'll sing and give God thanks after the promise comes to pass." Instead, they started singing the phrase over and over. Then they dug out the well, and suddenly, right in the middle of the desert, water began to shoot up out of it. They saw the promise they were given fulfilled.

Spring Up

There are promises God has put in you. Every circumstance may try to convince you it's not going to happen — you'll never get well, never get out of debt, never meet the right person. It's been a long time; you feel like you're in a drought. You must do like they did and sing to the promise. Your praise, your thanksgiving, and your declaration of faith are what cause water to flow in the desert.

It doesn't take any faith to sing after the water shows up; it's easy to sing after the promise is fulfilled. But the singing, the praise, is what causes

Your praise, your thanksgiving, and your declaration of faith are what cause water to flow in the desert.

JOEL OSTEEN

healing to spring up, abundance to spring up, breakthroughs to spring up. Sometimes we're waiting on God, but God's waiting on us. Why don't you start calling forth those promises that He's put in you?

If you're facing sickness, dare to say, "Spring up, healing. Lord, thank You that You're restoring health unto me." If you don't have the funds you need, "Spring up, abundance; spring up, promotion; spring up, opportunity; spring up, talent and creativity."

Perhaps you've been single for a long time and you're believing for a spouse, "Spring up, good-looking spouse." Maybe you're believing for children, "Spring up, baby; spring up, offspring. Father, You said my seed would be mighty in the land. You said that children are a gift from the Lord. I thank You that my child is on the way." You must sing to the promise, and it doesn't matter if you think your voice is good or not. You are singing to your circumstance not for others to hear.

Compaq Center

When we were believing to acquire the former Compaq Center as Lakewood's campus, all the odds were against us. Well-known business leaders told us we'd never get it, that we were wasting our time. We didn't have the connections, the money, the experience. All we had was a promise that we knew God put in our hearts.

Victoria and I would go up to the Compaq Center late at night when nothing was going on and walk around the building in the dark. With every step we would say, "Father thank You that You're fighting our battles. Thank You that You're bigger than these opponents. Thank You that You're making a way where we don't see a way." We were singing to the promise. We were saying in effect, "Spring up, Compaq Center. Spring up, destiny; spring up, favor. Spring up, breakthroughs." God supernaturally opened the door, and we're in the building today.

Be encouraged, you and God are a majority. If you'll stay full of faith, sing to that promise, and tell it to spring forth, all the forces of darkness cannot stop you. God has the final say. When He hears you singing — thanking Him before the answer comes, praising Him while you're in a drought, declaring His favor when the odds are against you — He'll make things happen you could never make happen. He'll open doors that no man can shut.

It's easy to complain about how it's not going to work out and talk about how impossible it is. That's going to cause you to live discouraged and settle for mediocrity. Why don't you start singing to the promise? There are goals God has put in you — dreams, healing, promotion, restoration — and they're lying dormant. You don't see how it could happen. You could easily settle there and think, *It's not meant to be.*

Those promises are still alive. You must start calling them out. "Healing, spring up in me. Talent, spring up in me. Abundance, spring up; good relationships, joy, and peace, spring up." All through the day, "Lord, thank You that my healing is coming. Thank You that opportunity, divine connections, the right people are in my future." You may be sick, but you can sing your way to healing. You may be discouraged, but you can sing your way to joy. You may be stuck in your career, but you can sing your way to the next level and see that dream come to pass.

Declaration Prayer of Promise

Heavenly Father,

Thank You for the promises You have placed within me. Despite the circumstances that surround me, I choose to lift my voice in praise. During what feels like a prolonged drought, I declare that I will sing to the promises You've planted in my heart. I recognize that my praise, thanksgiving, and steady faith are the catalysts for Your blessings in my life.

Lord, in areas where sickness lingers, I boldly declare, "Spring up, healing!" Thank You for restoring health unto me. In times of financial lack, I declare, "Spring up, abundance; spring up, promotion; spring up, opportunity; spring up, talent and creativity." I commit to continually sing to these promises, knowing that Your perfect timing is at work, and my breakthroughs are on the horizon.

In Jesus' name, amen.

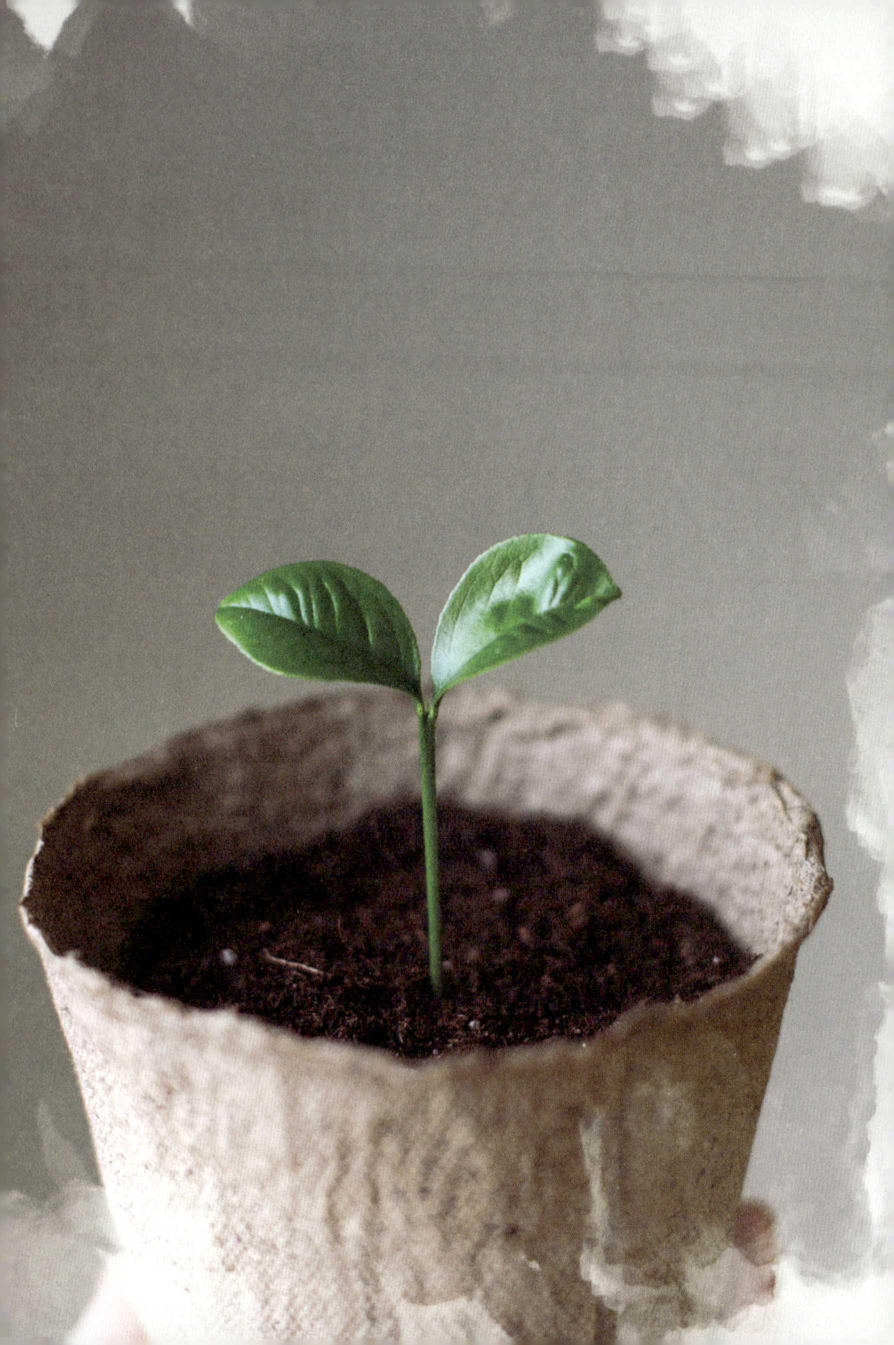

CHAPTER 14

Sing in Faith

"Sing, barren woman, you who never bore a child; burst into song, shout for joy, you who were never in labor; because more are the children of the desolate woman than of her who has a husband," says the LORD.

ISAIAH 54:1 (NIV)

Don't Wait

Too often, we think, *I'll wait until I see the promise, then I'll sing.* Then I'll thank God. But that's backward; you must sing first. You must make declarations of faith when you're in the drought, when the medical report is not good, when you don't know where the finances are coming from. That's when you must sing to the promise.

Unfruitful?

That's the truth Isaiah had in mind when he said, *"Sing, O barren woman, you who never bore a child. Break forth into song."* Isaiah wasn't writing this to women who had children. He didn't say, "Sing because God blessed you with the promise. Sing because the problem turned around." No, this encouragement was written to the women who had not yet seen the blessing of a baby.

Back in those days, if a woman didn't give her husband a child, she was looked down on and seen as second class. She was shamed and discredited. That's why you read in the Bible about people like Hannah; she was so distressed because she couldn't have a baby that she went to the altar and wept and wept, so much that the priest Eli thought she was drunk.

Isaiah wasn't talking to people who already had their promise. He was addressing those who were still barren. Still waiting for the promise. That could mean still believing for healing. Still hoping to meet the right person. Still standing in faith for that business to turn around.

What are you supposed to do when your "womb" isn't fruitful? Beg God to help you? Complain about how long it's taking? Get discouraged because life hasn't treated you fairly? No, when you are unfruitful and waiting for the breakthrough, Isaiah said, "Sing, break out into song."

The Birth Position

Here's the key: think of singing a song of praise as getting into the birth position. Thanking God is what causes the promise to come to pass. Complaining, being discouraged, and dwelling on your circumstances will keep you barren. But when you begin to praise, say, "Lord, I thank You for Your goodness in my life, thank You for Your favor. I know You didn't bring me this far to leave me. So thank You for new levels. Thank You for new opportunities. Thank You that I will become everything You've created me to be."

That's not just being grateful; that's getting yourself into the right position to give birth. If you continue to live with an attitude of praise, you'll give birth to the promise God put in your heart.

When we're barren, it's easy to get discouraged, become sour, and have a pity party. But when you start singing, when you start thanking God that things are changing in your favor, you can imagine God saying to the angels, "What's that sound I'm hearing? Most people would be upset and complaining, but listen to what they're saying. They're thanking Me that the answer is on the way. They're singing about the victory before they've seen the victory. Angels, go to work, open new doors, restore their health, turn that situation around, bring that dream to pass!"

Psalm 22:3 says that God inhabits the praises of His people. If you want God to reveal Himself, don't complain, don't talk about the problem; thank Him for His goodness, and sing to the promise. When you sing praise to God, you are not only putting yourself

When you sing praise to God, you are not only putting yourself in a position to give birth to new life, breakthroughs, healing, or that creative idea; you are creating an atmosphere for God to be there with you.

JOEL OSTEEN

in a position to give birth to new life, breakthroughs, healing, or that creative idea; you are creating an atmosphere for God to be there with you.

Are You Expecting?

That's what a young lady I know did. She and her husband had been trying to have a baby for a long time. They had spent a fortune on all the fertility treatments. Eventually, they were told they couldn't have children. But she didn't get discouraged. She didn't start complaining. Every day she would thank God that her baby was on the way. She did this year after year.

The promise God put in you is like a seed. And that seed must be watered. The way you water it is through your praise — by thanking God that it's coming, by having an attitude of expectancy. The reason some people stay barren and don't see the promise fulfilled is that they never water the seed.

They're excited in the beginning. They believe they're going to get well or meet the right person or get out of debt. The seed is planted, but when time goes by and they don't see anything happening, they quit watering it. If you plant an apple seed and never water it, it's not going to grow. There's nothing wrong with the seed. It's full of life. It has potential. It's just lacking water.

The promise God put in you may not have come to pass yet. It may seem like it's taking a long time. The good news is that the promise seed is still alive. It just needs some water. You may have to water it for a month, a year, or twenty years, but if you keep watering that seed, thanking God for the promise, it will come to pass at the appointed time.

This young lady and her husband kept watering their promise year after year. Then one day they stopped me in the church lobby to share some news. After nine years of waiting and watering, they were expecting a baby. Today they have a little boy and another baby on the way. This is after all the medical reports said that it wouldn't happen. *Couldn't* happen! The doctor was puzzled. He said, "I've never seen this before. Something happened, and your womb just opened."

As I write these words, she's close to forty years old. Recently her doctor told her, "You're physically like a twenty-year-old. You can probably have five more children." She laughed and said, "No, thanks, I don't want to be *that* blessed."

God can bring water out of an empty well. He can make streams in the desert. And He certainly can help you give birth to the promise within you. Sing to the promise. Thank God that it's on the way. Under your breath, make declarations of faith, "Spring up, O baby; spring up, breakthrough; spring up, health; spring up abundance!" When you give voice to an attitude of expectancy — when you're always watering that seed — God can and will do things that seemed impossible.

Declaration Prayer of Promise

Heavenly Father,

I come before Your throne with praise on my lips. I declare that my heart is a fertile ground, ready to receive the promises You have planted within me. I choose not to be discouraged or complain, but instead, I lift my voice in thanks for the goodness You have in store for me. With an attitude of expectancy, I declare that the promises, like seeds, will be watered by my praise, and I trust that they will come to pass in Your appointed time.

Lord, let my heart be filled with an unwavering belief that, despite the passage of time, Your promises are still alive, and I will give birth to them. May I sing to the promises and create an atmosphere where You are present, making the impossible a reality.

I declare breakthroughs, healing, and abundance over every aspect of my life and my family's lives. I trust that You can make streams in the desert and bring forth life where it seemed impossible.

In Jesus' name, amen.

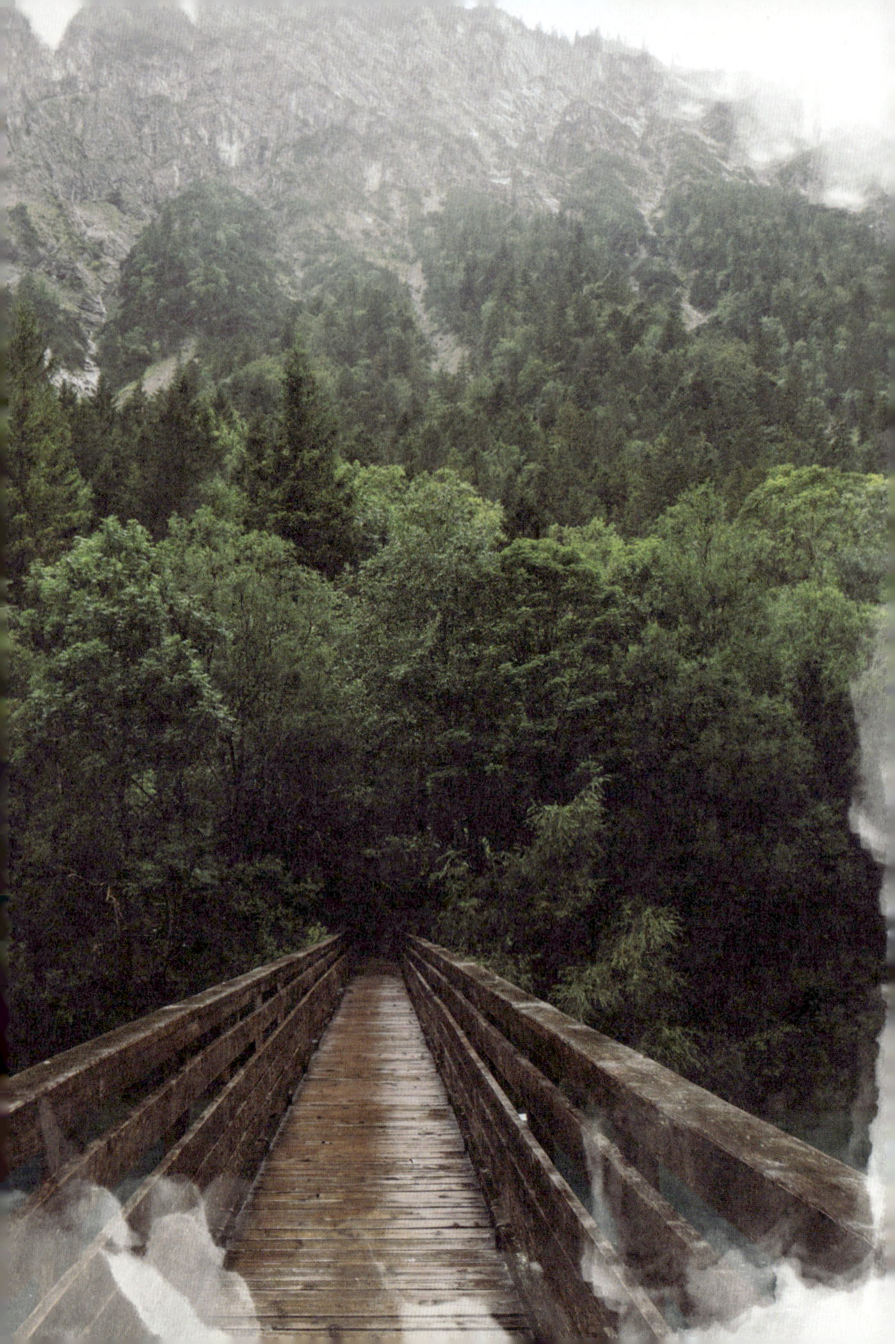

CHAPTER 15

He's Got You

But the Lord is faithful. He will establish you and guard you against the evil one.

2 THESSALONIANS 3:3 (ESV)

Director

God is directing your steps down to the smallest details. He can make things happen that you could never make happen on your own. He is for you. He is on your side. And what He has purposed for your life will come to pass.

I like what my friend Joyce Meyer says. She told someone, "I've been walking with God for twenty years." Then she heard the Holy Spirit say to her on the inside, "Excuse Me. You've been *walking* with Me for two years. I've been dragging you the other eighteen."

He Is in Control

God is so good, so loving, and so forgiving. Even if He must drag us, He will still get us to our destiny. We shouldn't look down on ourselves because we don't think we have enough faith or go around stressed out because it's not happening on our timetable. We can stay in peace, knowing that our God, the Creator of the universe, is in complete control.

God has already lined up your destiny moments, where you will see His hand of favor. A problem you've had for years will suddenly turn around. An opportunity of a lifetime will suddenly appear in front of you. These are destiny moments that God already has in your future.

God works in mysterious ways, far beyond anything we can understand. He knows how to draw people to you and align them with your cause. Why don't you trust Him? Why don't you believe that in your future these destiny moments await? You may not be able to make them happen, but He will! He's in complete control, and He promised to establish you.

Already Blessed

Numbers 23:11 (NLT) says, *Then King Balak demanded of Balaam, "What have you done to me? I brought you to curse my enemies. Instead, you have blessed them!"* Balaam replied, *"I received a command to bless; God has blessed, and I cannot reverse it!"* (v. 20). He could not curse what God had already blessed.

Get that down in your spirit. When God created you, He breathed His blessing into you. You have the DNA of Almighty God. Royal blood is flowing through your veins. You are wearing God's crown of favor. What God has blessed no person can curse.

Maybe somebody is talking about you. Your attitude should be, *No big deal. They are powerless to stop God's blessing on my life.* Well, maybe you got some bad breaks, you got laid off. *Yes, that's true, but I'm not worried about it. I know the blessing always overrides the curse.* Well, maybe you came from a rough family. You had a rough background. *That's all right, where I am is not where I'm staying. I know the blessing of God will get me to where I'm supposed to be.*

You Are Protected

I met a young lady who grew up in Rwanda. She and her family are strong believers. At twenty-two years of age, she came home from college for Easter break. At the time, there were two main tribes in Rwanda, who both considered themselves Rwandans. These two tribes had gotten along peacefully for many years. But one day, the president of the nation was killed, and rebels from one tribe started killing people from the opposing tribe, resulting in a horrific genocide. They went on a rampage, going from town to town ruthlessly slaughtering men, women, and children from the opposing tribe. Some of the

I know the blessing of God will get me to where I'm supposed to be.

JOEL OSTEEN

attackers were people this young lady had grown up with, played with, and even welcomed into her home.

Her parents were able to sneak her into a home of a pastor they knew — a Godly man who belonged to the attacking tribe. There she and six other girls hid in a small bathroom for many weeks, never making a sound; never coughing, talking, or even whispering. Imagine it: seven terrified individuals in a three-foot-by-four-foot bathroom.

Numerous times in those weeks, men from the attacking tribe knocked on the pastor's door, calling for her by name. Each time the pastor said, "She's not in here!" One time they forced their way in and searched the house. At one point, a man even had his hand on the doorknob of the bathroom where they were hiding. But just before he turned it, something distracted him and he walked away.

For 91 days, she stayed in that bathroom, never leaving once. She went in weighing 120 pounds. She came out weighing 70 pounds. During those three months, her parents, her relatives, and nearly one million other Rwandans were killed in this senseless genocide.

But the Lord is faithful. He will establish you and guard you against the evil one.

2 THESSALONIANS 3:3 (ESV)

But the Lord is
faithful. He will
establish you and
guard you against
the evil one.

2 THESSALONIANS 3:3 (ESV)

Here's what I want you to take away from this otherwise sad story. If it's not your time to go, all the forces of darkness cannot stop you from living. What God has purposed for your life will come to pass. God is bigger than any enemy, bigger than any injustice, bigger than any sickness.

The Scripture says when the Enemy comes in like a flood, the spirit of God will raise up a delivering, protecting, rescuing barrier. God knows how to protect you. Just as God can make blind eyes see, He can make seeing eyes blind. God can shield you from the Enemy.

Today, this beautiful young lady works for the United Nations. She goes around the world telling her story, letting people know that when you believe, all things are possible. When you don't see a way, God can make a way. When it looks like it's over, God has the final say. God has you in the palm of His hand.

So, come back to that place of peace. There is a hedge of protection around you that the Enemy cannot cross. And what is meant for your harm, God said He would use to your advantage.

Failure Is Not an Option

Shake off every disappointment and negative comment people have made. Shake off self-pity and put on a new, faith-filled attitude because God's got you. Get up every morning and say, "Father, thank You that Your destiny for me will come to pass. Thank You that I will leave my mark on this generation." Always remember this: No one can successfully curse you because God has already blessed you. If you have this attitude of faith, obey God, and honor Him with your life, you're going to come into your promise. His favor will thrust you to new levels. I believe and declare over you that you will see God's purpose come to pass in your life. You will overcome every obstacle, defeat every enemy, and become everything God has created you to be!

Declaration Prayer of Promise

Heavenly Father,

I praise You for being so good and loving, and for lining up my destiny moments. I shake off every disappointment and negative word spoken against me. I thank You for Your protection and declare my new, faith-filled attitude because I trust in Your plan for me.

Thank You for assuring me that Your destined purpose will come to pass and I will leave a positive mark on this generation. I declare that, before any curse, You have already blessed me. With faith, obedience, and a life honoring You, I step into the promises and favor You have for me, overcoming obstacles and becoming all You've created me to be.

In Jesus' name, amen.

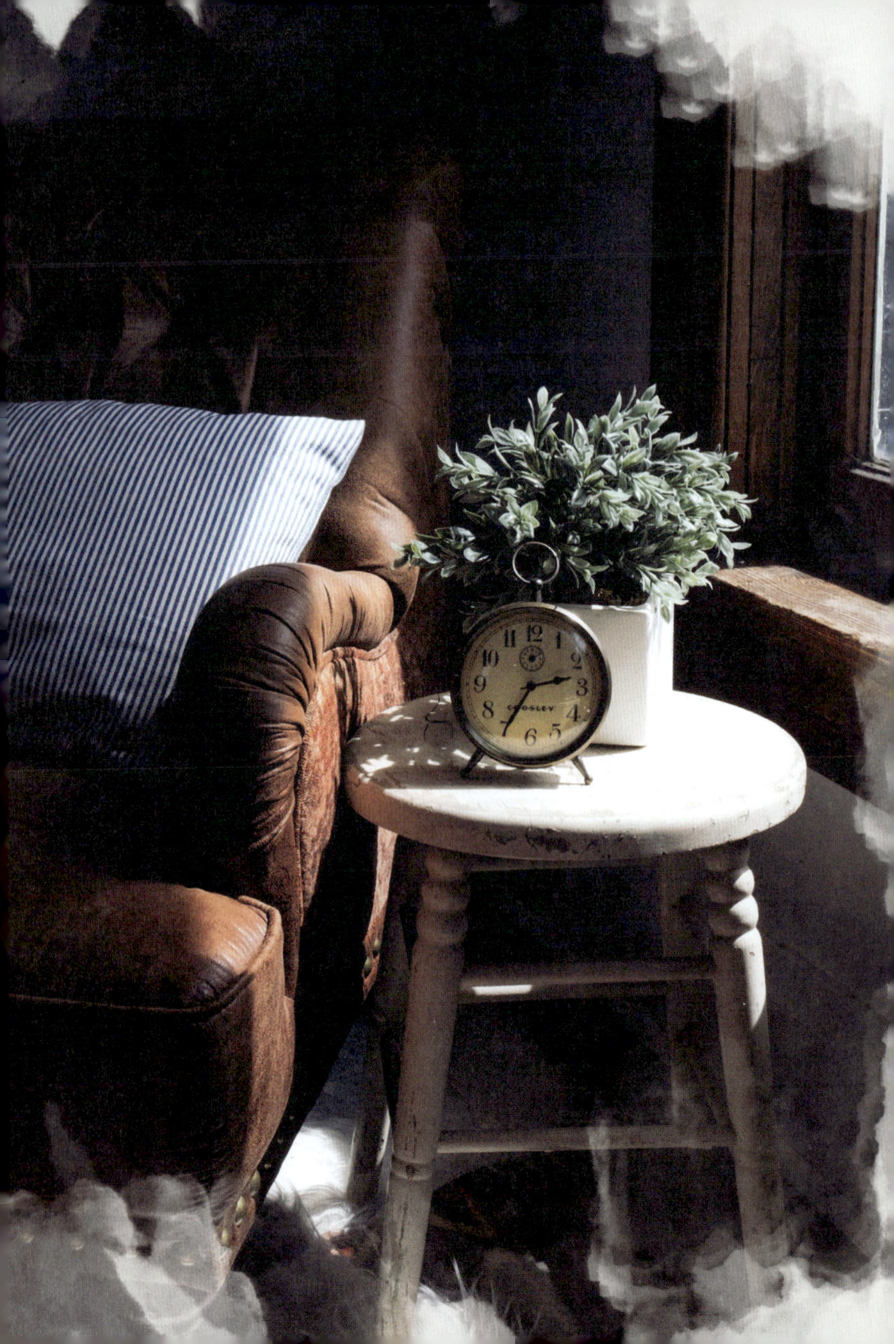

CHAPTER 16
It's Time

"For I know the plans I have for you," says the LORD. "They are plans for good and not for disaster, to give you a future and a hope."

JEREMIAH 29:11 (NLT)

Designer

God sees the end from the beginning. He holds in His loving Father-heart all the details of the good plans He designed for your destiny and is orchestrating on your behalf. He knows all the days of your life.

Plans are the thoughts, intentions, projects, and purposes God has for us. This means God has the big picture and all the detailed schematics about your destiny.

As you follow the encouragement I've shared in these pages, you will see blessing, favor, influence, and opportunities like you've never seen. Don't let negative thoughts keep you from where you are going. Start believing your dreams are not only possible but promised and about to come to pass.

I Made the Plans

It's easy to forget how much power God has. Every aspect of our lives, down to the smallest detail, has already been planned out and foreseen. God loves to line up the right people to come across your path and arrange the right breaks for your future. He loves to create solutions in advance to every problem that you will ever face.

The Scripture says, *"For the LORD of hosts has purposed, and who will annul it?"* (Isaiah 14:27, NKJV). This is saying God has a purpose for your life. He's already planned out your days. Then it asks the question: Who will annul it? God is saying, "Who can stop My plan? Who is more powerful than Me? I created the millions of galaxies, every star in them, and gave each a name just so you can see how big I am. Now, who can have a dream so great that I can't bring it to pass?"

You Can't Be Canceled

God's plan and purpose for you cannot be stopped by a setback, an illness, or the opinions of others. No force of darkness can prevent you from reaching your destiny. Sometimes, we may believe that our mistakes or current life circumstances have derailed God's plan. You're not that powerful.

Yes, you may have made mistakes, but they weren't a surprise to God. His mercy has already covered it all. Why not shake off the guilt and move forward? Nothing you've done or haven't done has canceled your destiny.

You Can't Cancel Yourself

I received a letter one time from a lady who had survived a car accident, which broke her neck. After months of her husband taking care of her post-surgery, she convinced him to return to work. Then one day, overwhelmed by depression and pain, she decided to end her life.

Her husband was a big hunter and had a gun rack over in the corner of the living room. She couldn't walk over there by herself and decided to crawl. But when she got out of the chair, she lost her balance, knocked over the end table, and fell flat on her back, unable to move.

Interestingly, the remote control for the television hit the floor and the batteries came out. When it did, it changed the channel on the television. It just so happened to go to a station where I was ministering. Her first thought was, *Oh, great, I'm dying. Now I've got to listen to this TV preacher to add to my misery.*

That day, I was talking about how God can turn any situation around. How He can take your darkest hour and turn it into your brightest hour. She began to feel a peace like she'd never felt before. In her letter to me, she said, "I couldn't move my body. I couldn't open my eyes. But I could feel tears of joy running down my cheeks. That moment was a turning point." Today, several years later, she's happy, healthy, whole, and on the way to fulfilling her destiny.

You are not powerful enough to stop God's plan. Your days have already been recorded and numbered by the Creator of the universe. It's time to believe and receive those plans. You can be the happiest you have ever been, regardless of what is happening around you. It's time to dream again. Rest assured; you are safe in the hands of the Designer.

Officer Stabbed

I read a newspaper article that reported a police officer being attacked and stabbed in the head by a man high on drugs. The three-and-a-half-inch knife blade went straight into his brain. He was rushed to the hospital, and his family was informed that he was most likely brain-dead. Even if he did survive, he would never be able to walk or talk.

When all the X-rays came back, the doctor was amazed. The blade missed the part of the brain that controls motor skills by less than a millimeter, or .039 inches. It missed the part of the brain that controls speech by less than a millimeter. It missed the main nerve that gives sensation by less than a millimeter. It missed the main artery that supplies blood to the brain by less than a millimeter.

The surgeon said, "It is unbelievable. The only way I can describe it is he was less than .04 inches away from death in every direction. A fraction this way, he'd be dead, and a fraction that way, totally incapacitated."

God Is in Complete Control

Friend, nothing can snatch you out of God's hand. Know and believe that right now God is working behind the scenes, arranging things in your favor. He's making a way where you don't see a way. You don't have to live worried, stressed out, trying to force everything to happen. All you've got to do is keep God first, obey Him, and honor Him with your life, and you will come into these destiny moments where you see God supernaturally protecting you.

Ready to Dream Again?

It's time. After reading this book, are you ready to dream again? I have shared with you how to navigate through challenges and stay on track to the fulfillment of your dream. There is nothing that can detour or prevent God from leading you to the promise He gave you. Now is the time. Today is the day for you to start dreaming again. Your destiny is waiting for you.

Get out of your despair, remember what He said, shake the dirt off the once-buried treasure, and embrace the right images of yourself. Imagine the possibilities. Sing to the promise. And know you are not a grasshopper; you are an eagle.

So, go soar above your circumstances with God and dream big. Your dream will happen.

Declaration Prayer of Promise

Heavenly Father,

You know every dream in my heart and every promise You've made. I trust You enough to believe You will bring every promise that You've spoken to me to fulfillment at the right time in my due season.

I am so grateful for Your unfailing goodness and love. I declare that Your divine plan and purpose for my life are unstoppable, unaffected by setbacks, sickness, or the opinions of others. I shake off any disappointment, negative words, or self-pity and put on a new, faith-filled attitude as I trust in Your sovereign plan for my life.

Thank You for the assurance that Your destined purpose for my life will come to pass, and I will leave a positive mark on this generation. I reject any notion that my mistakes can derail Your plan, acknowledging that Your mercy covers it all, and I move forward free from guilt.

I trust in You; I believe You're arranging things in my favor, making a way where I don't see a way. I step into the promises and favor You have for me and believe I am becoming who You've created me to be.

As I embrace the encouragements in this book, I declare a renewed ability to dream again. Today is the day for me to start dreaming big. To shake off despair. To embrace Your promises and soar above my circumstances on wings of faith.

In Jesus' name, I declare this. Amen.

Stay encouraged *and* inspired all through the week.

Download the Joel Osteen Daily Podcast *and* subscribe now *on* YouTube to get the latest videos.

For a full listing, visit JoelOsteen.com/How-To-Watch.

SiriusXM Apple Podcasts **Spotify** YouTube **ROKU**

Stay connected, *be* blessed.

Get more from Joel & Victoria Osteen

It's time to step into the life of victory and favor that God has planned for you! Featuring new messages from Joel & Victoria Osteen, their free daily devotional and inspiring articles, hope is always at your fingertips with the free Joel Osteen app and online at JoelOsteen.com.

Get the app and visit us today at JoelOsteen.com.

Download on the **App Store** | GET IT ON **Google Play**

Joel — JOEL OSTEEN MINISTRIES

CONNECT WITH US